GET
CRACKING!™

Photographs: Tango Photographie
Food stylist: Renée Girard
Recipe preparation: Jacques Faucher
Graphic design: Zapp

Pictured on the front cover: Egg, Tomato and Cheese Salad (see page 64)

Published by Brimar Publishing Inc.
338 Saint Antoine Street East
Montreal, Canada H2Y 1A3
Tel. (514) 954-1441
Fax (514) 954-5086

Please forward any requests, questions or comments to:
Canadian Egg Marketing Agency
112 Kent Street, Suite 1501
Ottawa, Ontario K1P 5P2

Canadä
The publisher thanks Heritage Canada for the support awarded under the
Book Publishing Industry Development Program.

ISBN: 2-89433-457-5

Printed in Canada

GET CRACKING!™

BRIMAR

Introduction

Make eggs part of your healthy lifestyle!

Start your day sunny-side up. Breakfast is the most important meal of the day. Even if you've only got a minute, you've got time to scramble an egg in a mug or roll up a tortilla for the road.

But eggs aren't just for breakfast! A good source of protein, eggs can be used in dozens of creative ways. Breakfast, brunch, lunch, dinner and snacks, they can be served anytime.

Add a little sunshine to those lunchtime blues with a Sliced Egg Sandwich, a Bagel & Egg Melt or an Egg Pizza Roll-Up.

Prepare main dishes with ease and flair. Try egg-inspired pastas, fajitas, quiches, pizzas, soups and soufflés.

Eggs are not only wholesome, versatile and delicious, they are a nutritious, economical meal solution.

With over 115 recipes, from basic cooking techniques to *eggs*traordinary meal ideas, the *Get Cracking* cookbook contains recipes for all occasions.

So, Get Cracking with these *egg*citing recipes and make the most of the grade "A" goodness of eggs.

Contents

*Egg*cellent Nutrition

Eggs are one of nature's most nutritious foods. One large egg contains a wide range of vitamins and minerals and only 75 calories.

One grade "A" large egg (50 g) provides:

Energy		75 kilocalories (310 kilojoules)
Protein		6 g
Fat		5 g
	Polyunsaturates	0.8 g
	Monounsaturates	2.0 g
	Saturates	1.5 g
Cholesterol		190 mg *
Carbohydrate		0.5 g

* 1999 nutrient analysis indicates that cholesterol values have dropped from 215 mg, as previously reported in the 1991 Canadian Nutrient File.

Eggs contain all nine essential amino acids, making them an excellent, and affordable, source of high-quality protein. Protein is essential for building and repairing body tissue. Muscles, organs, skin and hair as well as antibodies, enzymes and hormones are all made from protein.

Handling Eggs

Buying

To ensure top quality, buy only grade "A" eggs that have been kept refrigerated and that have clean, oval, uncracked shells.

All eggs sold in grocery stores are grade "A" eggs. These eggs also have a firm white, a small air cell at the wide end and a centered yolk. In other words, grade "A" eggs are fresh, high-quality eggs!

When buying eggs, check the "Best Before" date on the carton. It indicates the length of time the eggs will maintain their grade "A" quality. If you want to eat them after that date, they are best used in thoroughly cooked dishes, i.e., baked, hard-cooked or scrambled rather than soft-poached or fried.

Chilling

Eggs are perishable. When shopping, pick up eggs last. Ask the cashier to pack them with frozen items to keep them cold longer. Get them home and into a refrigerator immediately.

Keep eggs as fresh as possible by storing them in the refrigerator in their original carton. The carton protects the eggs from absorbing flavors and odors of other foods nearby, especially from strong-smelling foods like onions, cheese or cabbage. Keep raw foods (meats, poultry and eggs) separate from cooked foods in the refrigerator.

Leftover raw egg whites and raw yolks should be put in airtight containers and stored in the refrigerator immediately. To prevent yolks from drying up, cover them with a little cold water. Drain the water before using. Hard-cooked eggs should also be refrigerated.

Freezing

Raw eggs can be frozen. Lightly beat whole eggs just until blended. Pour them into a freezer container, seal tightly, label with the number of eggs and the date, and freeze. Substitute 3 tbsp (45 mL) thawed whole eggs for 1 large fresh egg. Eggs should not be frozen in the shell.

Egg whites can be frozen "as is." Pour them into a freezer container, seal tightly, label with the number of egg whites and the date, and freeze. Substitute 2 tbsp (30 mL) thawed egg whites for 1 large egg white.

Egg yolks will thicken or gel when frozen and therefore cannot be used in a recipe unless they receive special treatment. To prevent this gelation, beat in either 1/8 tsp (0.5 mL) salt or 1 1/2 tsp (7 mL) sugar or corn syrup per 1/4 cup (50 mL) egg yolks (about 4 yolks). Label with the number of yolks, the date and whether you added salt (for main dishes) or sugar (for desserts or baking). Substitute 1 tbsp (15 mL) thawed yolks for 1 large fresh yolk.

Freeze eggs in small quantities and defrost only what you need. An easy way to freeze them is to put them in an ice cube tray. When frozen, transfer to a freezer container and label.

It is best to thaw eggs in the refrigerator and use them as soon as they are thawed. Use them only in dishes that will be thoroughly cooked.

STORAGE TIMES

	Refrigerator	Freezer
Whole raw eggs	Use by "Best Before" date	4 months (beaten)
Raw yolks or whites	2 to 4 days	4 months
Hard-cooked eggs	1 week	Not recommended

Cooking

After removing eggs from the refrigerator, use them immediately. To prevent toughness, always use moderate heat and controlled cooking times for eggs.

Eggs are used in a wide variety of ways and are an essential part of cooking. They can bind ingredients, as in meatloaves or croquettes. They can also leaven baked high-rises such as soufflés and sponge cakes. Their thickening ability is seen in custards and sauces. They emulsify mayonnaise, salad dressings and hollandaise sauce and are frequently used to coat or glaze breads and cookies. They clarify soups and coffee. In boiled candies and frostings, they delay crystallization. As a finishing touch, they can be hard-cooked and used as a garnish.

Substituting Egg Sizes

All of the recipes in this book have been tested using large eggs. If you need to substitute eggs of other sizes for large eggs, use the chart below.

If a recipe calls for... You can use...

	Extra Large	Medium	Small
1 large egg	1	1	2
2 large eggs	2	2	3
3 large eggs	3	4	4
4 large eggs	3	5	6
5 large eggs	4	6	7
6 large eggs	5	7	8

Serving

When entertaining, serve all egg dishes within two hours. Cold egg dishes and beverages should be kept on ice. Serve eggs and egg-rich foods immediately after cooking, or refrigerate and use within three to four days.

Egg Tips

- If a recipe calls for eggs at room temperature, immerse them in warm water for a few minutes.
- Grade "A" Jumbo, Extra Large, Large, Medium, Small and Pee Wee eggs are determined by weight, not by the physical size of the egg.
- Don't be fooled by the color of eggshells. Color is not related to quality, flavor or nutritional value. The breed of hen determines the color of the eggshell.
- Eggs with a visible blood spot on the yolk are suitable for consumption. The spot can be removed with the tip of a knife, if desired.
- If you're taking deviled eggs or other perishable foods to a picnic, pack them with ice or a commercial coolant in an insulated bag or cooler to keep them cold (at 40°F/4°C or lower).
- At Easter time, eggs are handled a great deal more than usual. If you won't be coloring hard-cooked eggs right after cooking them, store the eggs in their cartons in the refrigerator. Don't color cracked eggs or use them for an egg hunt. If your colored eggs will be eaten later, be sure to use only food coloring to decorate them.
- Don't eat cracked eggs or eggs that have been out of the refrigerator for more than two hours.

BASIC TECHNIQUES

Whether hard-cooked, microwaved, fried, poached, scrambled, in meringues or in soufflés...all you need to know about cooking with the marvelous egg!

Eggs in the Shell

Preparation: 2 minutes
Cooking: 10 minutes
Standing: 25 minutes

- Place cold eggs in a single layer in a saucepan. Cover with cold water reaching at least 1 inch (2.5 cm) above the top of the eggs.

- Cover saucepan and bring quickly to a boil over high heat. Immediately remove pan from heat to stop boiling.

- Let eggs stand in water 20 to 25 minutes for hard-cooked eggs, or 1 to 4 minutes for soft-cooked eggs.

- Drain water and immediately run cold water over eggs until cooled.

- To peel a hard-cooked egg, crackle shell by tapping all over, then roll the egg between your hands to loosen the shell. Begin peeling at the large end. Hold the egg under cold running water or dip in a bowl of water to help ease off the shell.

TIPS: Use eggs that have been in the refrigerator the longest because less fresh eggs are easier to peel. Peel eggs soon after cooking and cooling.

Before cooking, prick large end of eggs with a pin to prevent them from cracking.

Cool eggs quickly once the cooking time is up by placing in cold water. Rapid cooling helps prevent a green ring from forming around the yolk.

To determine whether an egg is hard-cooked, spin it. If it spins around and around, it is hard-cooked. If it wobbles and will not spin, it is raw.

Use hard-cooked eggs within one week.

Nutrients per serving (2 eggs)
Calories: 148
Protein: 12.4 g
Carbohydrate: 1.2 g
Fat: 10.0 g

Pickled Eggs

Makes 6 pickled eggs
Preparation: 10 minutes
Cooking: 10 minutes

6	hard-cooked eggs, peeled	6
1/2 cup	vinegar	125 mL
1 cup	water	250 mL
1 tsp	sugar	5 mL
3/4 tsp	salt	3 mL
1/2 tsp	peppercorns	2 mL
5	whole cloves	5
1/2	bay leaf	1/2
1	dried chili pepper	1

Nutrients per serving (2 eggs)
Calories: 154
Protein: 12.4 g
Carbohydrate: 2.6 g
Fat: 10.0 g

- Place hard-cooked eggs in a jar. In a small saucepan, combine other ingredients.
- Cover and bring to a boil. Simmer for 10 minutes over low heat.
- Strain liquid and cool to room temperature.
- Cover eggs with vinegar solution. Cover with lid and let stand in the refrigerator for at least 2 days before using.

TIP: Pickled eggs will keep several months without refrigeration if the container is unopened. Once opened, refrigerate and use within one month.

Variation: Super-Easy Pickled Eggs – Drop peeled hard-cooked eggs into pickle juice. Refrigerate several days before using.

Egg Salad

Makes 4 servings
Preparation: 10 minutes

6	hard-cooked eggs, peeled and coarsely chopped	6
2 tbsp	regular or light mayonnaise (or yogurt)	30 mL
1/4 cup	chopped green onions	50 mL
2 tsp	Dijon mustard (or to taste)	10 mL
	garlic powder, hot pepper sauce and salt, to taste	

- In a bowl, combine eggs, mayonnaise (or yogurt), onions and mustard. Add garlic powder, hot pepper sauce and salt.
- Use as directed for one of the variations.

Nutrients per serving
Calories: 166
Protein: 9.7 g
Carbohydrate: 1.6 g
Fat: 13.1 g

TIPS: If you are making egg salad for a large group of people, mash the eggs with a pastry blender or potato masher, or run them through a food mill.

If you need hard-cooked eggs in a hurry for a salad, crack the eggs into a poacher and cook them until they reach the desired doneness. Immerse eggs in cold water for rapid cooling.

Variations: Honey-Dijon Egg Salad Sandwiches – Use Honey-Dijon mustard to make basic Egg Salad; add 3/4 cup (175 mL) chopped dill pickles. Place a slice of ham on each of 4 slices of rye or pumpernickel bread. Divide egg salad mixture between sandwiches and top with slices of bread. Serve immediately, or cover with plastic wrap and refrigerate.

Tex-Mex Egg Salad Sandwiches – To basic Egg Salad, add Tex-Mex seasoning or chili powder, to taste. Spread filling over four 6-inch (15 cm) flour or whole wheat tortillas. Sprinkle with 2 tbsp (30 mL) chopped fresh coriander or parsley. Roll up tightly. Serve immediately, or cover with plastic wrap and refrigerate. Serve with tomato salsa.

Scrambled Eggs

Makes 1 serving
Preparation: 2 minutes
Cooking: 2 minutes

2	eggs	2
2 tbsp	milk	30 mL
	salt and pepper, to taste	
1 tsp	butter	5 mL

Stovetop Directions

- Whisk together eggs, milk and seasonings.

- Heat a skillet over medium-high heat until hot enough to make a drop of water sizzle. Melt butter in skillet.

- Pour in egg mixture and immediately reduce heat to medium-low. As mixture begins to set, gently move spatula across bottom and sides of skillet to form large, soft curds.

- Cook until eggs are thickened but still moist, and no visible liquid egg remains.

Microwave Directions

- Whisk ingredients together in a microwaveable container (round containers work best for eggs). Cover with plastic wrap, leaving a small steam vent.

- Microwave on 'Medium-high' (70%) for 1 minute 30 seconds to 1 minute 45 seconds, stirring several times during cooking.

- Cover and let stand 30 seconds to 1 minute before serving. Eggs will look slightly moist, but will finish cooking upon standing, so do not overcook.

TIPS: Although it's best to serve scrambled eggs immediately after cooking, you can hold them for a short time by covering them and placing over a pan of hot water rather than placing over direct heat.

Slow cooking will give you perfect scrambled eggs that are fluffy, creamy and thick.

Variations: Scramble eggs with 1/2 cup (125 mL) shredded or cubed Cheddar or Mozzarella cheese.

Scramble eggs with 1/4 cup (50 mL) each well-drained mild salsa and shredded cheese.

Sauté 1 small zucchini and 1 small onion in 1 tbsp (15 mL) butter, until softened. Add 1 14-oz (398 mL) can spaghetti sauce with garden vegetables. Simmer for 5 minutes and set aside. Scramble 6 eggs with 1/3 cup (75 mL) milk. Spoon spaghetti sauce mixture over eggs. *Makes 6 servings.*

Melt 1 tsp (5 mL) butter in a skillet. Break 1 slice of bread into small pieces and add to skillet, stirring until golden. Add 1 or 2 eggs and scramble until set but not dry.

Nutrients per serving
Calories: 197
Protein: 13.5 g
Carbohydrate: 2.7 g
Fat: 14.3 g

Microwaved Eggs

Makes 1 serving
Preparation: 1 minute
Cooking: 1 1/2 minutes

1 tsp	butter	5 mL
2	eggs	2

- Divide butter between two coffee mugs, small dessert bowls or ramekins. Microwave on 'High' (100%) for about 15 seconds. Rotate bowls to butter all sides.

- Crack one egg into each bowl. Pierce egg yolk with a toothpick or fork. Cover with plastic wrap, with one corner pulled back for venting.

- Microwave on 'Medium-high' (70%) for 45 seconds to 1 minute, or until desired doneness is reached. Let stand 1 to 2 minutes without removing the plastic wrap.

TIPS: The microwave recipes used in this book were tested in a 700-watt microwave oven using the following power level designations:
High = 100%,
Medium-high = 70%,
Medium = 50%,
Medium-low = 30%.
Check your oven's instruction booklet to see which settings on your oven correspond to these terms. If you use a power level other than those listed above to cook the food in these recipes, the cooking times will be affected.

Always use microwave-safe cookware in your microwave oven. Glass, ceramic and plastic cookware are all microwave-safe. Plastic cookware gives the most even cooking since it doesn't attract as much heat away from the food as does glass or ceramic cookware.

Variations: Eggs in Potato Nests – Combine 1 cup (250 mL) shredded extra-old Cheddar cheese and 1 cup (250 mL) cooked hash brown potatoes. Divide mixture among 4 greased ramekins, making a nest. Crack 1 egg into each nest. Pierce egg yolk with a toothpick or fork. Microwave on 'Medium' (50%) for 5 minutes. Sprinkle with additional shredded cheese. Let stand for 3 to 4 minutes. *Makes 4 servings.*

Egg in a Basket – Line custard cup or ramekin with a crustless, buttered slice of bread. Break an egg into it. Pierce egg yolk with a toothpick or fork. Microwave on 'Medium' (50%) for 2 minutes. *Makes 1 serving.*

Egg in a Tomato – Cut a thick slice from the stem end of a medium-size tomato. Scoop out seeds and center pulp. Place tomato in a small bowl. Place 1/2 tsp (2 mL) butter in tomato. Break an egg into it. Pierce egg yolk with a toothpick or fork. Sprinkle 1 tbsp (15 mL) shredded Cheddar cheese over egg. Cover with top of tomato. Microwave on 'Medium-high' (70%) for 1 minute 45 seconds, or until egg is almost cooked. Let stand 1 minute. *Makes 1 serving.*

Nutrients per serving
Calories: 182
Protein: 12.4 g
Carbohydrate: 1.2 g
Fat: 13.6 g

Poached Eggs

Makes 1 serving
Preparation: 2 minutes
Cooking: 5 minutes

2	eggs	2

Stovetop Directions

- Bring 3 inches (8 cm) of water to a boil. Reduce to a gentle simmer.
- Break cold eggs, one at a time, into a small dish. Gently slip eggs into water.
- Cook in barely simmering water 3 to 5 minutes. Remove eggs with a slotted spoon and drain well.

Microwave Directions

- Pour 1/3 cup (75 mL) water into a small, deep bowl. Bring to a boil on 'High' (100%). Break eggs and slip into water.
- Pierce yolk membrane with a fork. Cover with plastic wrap, leaving a small steam vent. Cook on 'High' (100%) 40 to 60 seconds.
- Let stand, covered, 1 to 2 minutes. Drain and serve.

TIPS: A shallow saucepan with a large surface area is best for poaching eggs.

For poached eggs with a compact oval shape, use the freshest eggs available and add a few drops of vinegar to the water. Rapid boiling will cause eggs to break up as they cook.

Poached eggs can be made ahead of time and kept for up to two days. Undercook them slightly so that the yolks remain runny when reheated. Refrigerate, covered, or store in ice-cold water, deep enough to cover eggs, until ready to use. To complete cooking, immerse in barely simmering water 1 to 2 minutes.

Eggs can be poached in dry white wine, chicken broth or tomato juice.

Nutrients per serving
Calories: 148
Protein: 12.4 g
Carbohydrate: 1.2 g
Fat: 10.0 g

Eggs Benedict

Makes 4 servings
Preparation: 7 minutes
Cooking: 15 minutes

8	eggs	8
	water, dry white wine, chicken broth or tomato juice, to poach	
	a few drops of vinegar	
4	English muffins, split and toasted	4
8	slices of ham or cooked back bacon	8

Hollandaise Sauce

1/2 cup	butter, melted	125 mL
3	egg yolks	3
1 tbsp	lemon juice	15 mL
	pinch salt and cayenne pepper or dry mustard	

Nutrients per serving
Calories: 549
Protein: 23.1 g
Carbohydrate: 23.1 g
Fat: 40.2

Sauce (stovetop method)

- In top of double boiler, whisk together all sauce ingredients.
- Cook over simmering water, stirring constantly until thickened, 10 to 12 minutes.

Sauce (microwave method)

- In a 4-cup (1 L) glass measure, whisk together egg yolks, lemon juice and spices. Gradually whisk melted butter into egg yolk mixture, beating constantly.
- Microwave on 'Medium' (50%) for 30 seconds to 1 minute, or until sauce thickens. Whisk halfway through and at end of cooking to produce a smooth sauce. Serve warm.

- Poach eggs in selected liquid and vinegar as described on page 16.
- Top each toasted English muffin half with a slice of ham or cooked back bacon, a poached egg and 2 tbsp (30 mL) hollandaise sauce.

TIPS: Curdling of the hollandaise sauce may occur due to overbeating or adding butter too quickly. To rescue a curdled sauce, try one of the following: Beat another egg yolk in a small bowl; with a whisk or fork, gradually beat in the curdled hollandaise sauce. Alternatively, place 1 tbsp (15 mL) water in a small bowl; with a whisk or fork, beat in a small amount of separated sauce until it becomes smooth, and keep adding sauce slowly, while continuing to beat vigorously.

Hollandaise sauce may be frozen. To use, thaw in refrigerator. Warm in double boiler over hot (not boiling) water, stirring constantly. If sauce should separate, use procedure described above.

Deviled Eggs

Makes 24 appetizers
Preparation: 10 minutes

12	hard-cooked eggs, peeled	12
1/4 cup	regular or light mayonnaise	50 mL
2 tsp	Dijon mustard	10 mL
	salt and pepper, to taste	

- Cut eggs in half lengthwise and remove yolks. In a bowl, mash yolks with a fork, then add mayonnaise, mustard, salt and pepper.
- Divide yolk mixture in half. To each half, add the ingredients for one of the variations.
- Refill egg whites with egg yolk mixture and garnish to taste. Serve immediately or store, covered, in refrigerator. Use within 3 days.

TIPS: For a picnic, place the cooked egg white halves in a plastic container and the deviled yolk filling in a plastic bag. Place both in a cooler. When you are ready to serve, cut off one corner of the plastic bag and pipe the filling into the egg white halves.

Variations: With Herbs – To half of egg yolk mixture, add 1 tbsp (15 mL) each minced fresh chives and minced fresh parsley, and a pinch each dried tarragon and garlic powder. Garnish with cherry tomato wedges.

With Shrimp and Olives – To half of egg yolk mixture, add 1/4 cup (50 mL) mashed cooked shrimp, 1/4 cup (50 mL) chopped black olives and 1 tbsp (15 mL) minced fresh parsley. Add drained horseradish and lemon juice, to taste. Garnish with mayonnaise, small cooked shrimps and sliced black olives.

Nutrients per appetizer
Calories: 54
Protein: 3.2 g
Carbohydrate: 0.4 g
Fat: 4.4 g

1

Cut eggs in half
lengthwise and remove
yolks. Mash yolks with
a fork, then add
mayonnaise, mustard,
salt and pepper.

2

Divide yolk mixture in
half. To each half, add
the ingredients for one
of the variations.

3

Refill egg whites with
egg yolk mixture and
garnish.

1

Beat together eggs and water; season with salt and pepper.

2

As mixture sets at the edges, push cooked portions toward the center with a spatula.

3

Slip spatula under the unfilled side, fold the omelet in half and slide onto a warm plate.

French Omelet

Makes 1 serving
Preparation: 2 minutes
Cooking: 4 to 5 minutes

2	eggs	2
2 tbsp	water	30 mL
	salt and pepper, to taste	
1 tbsp	butter	15 mL
	filling, optional (see Variations)	

- In a bowl, beat together eggs and water; season with salt and pepper.
- In a skillet, melt butter over medium-high heat.
- Pour in egg mixture. As mixture sets at the edges, gently push cooked portions toward the center with a spatula. Tilt and rotate the pan to allow uncooked egg to flow into the empty spaces.
- When eggs are almost set on surface but still look moist, cover one half of the omelet with filling (if desired).
- Slip spatula under the unfilled side, fold the omelet in half and slide onto a warm plate.

Nutrients per serving
Calories: 250
Protein: 12.6 g
Carbohydrate: 1.2 g
Fat: 21.4 g

TIPS: Pan is hot enough when a drop of water will roll around instead of bursting into steam immediately.

The proper pan is important for successful omelet making. The right size pan for a 1-, 2- or 3-egg omelet is about 8 inches (20 cm) in diameter at the base. It should be shallow with sloping sides to make it easier to slide the omelet onto the plate.

Always prepare several individual omelets rather than one large one. You will find each will be lighter, fluffier and easier to handle. Multiply the recipe for as many servings as you need and use 1/2 cup (125 mL) egg mixture for each 2-egg omelet and 3/4 cup (175 mL) for each 3-egg omelet.

Variations: Western – In 2 tbsp (30 mL) melted butter, cook 1/4 cup (50 mL) finely chopped ham, 2 tbsp (30 mL) chopped green pepper and 1 tbsp (15 mL) finely chopped onion until vegetables are tender but not browned. Pour in omelet mixture and cook as directed.

Strawberry-Orange – Replace water in French Omelet recipe with orange juice. Cook as directed. Fill with 1/2 cup (125 mL) sliced fresh strawberries. Sprinkle omelet with icing sugar or garnish with a dollop of whipped cream.

Herbs – To omelet mixture, add 2 tbsp (30 mL) finely chopped fresh parsley, 1 tsp (5 mL) finely chopped green onion, 1/2 tsp (2 mL) dried tarragon and 1/8 tsp (0.5 mL) finely chopped garlic. Cook as directed.

Quiche Lorraine

Makes 6 servings
Preparation: 8 minutes
Cooking: 35 minutes
Standing: 5 minutes

1	pre-baked 9-inch (23 cm) pie shell	1
6	slices crisp bacon, crumbled	6
1 cup	shredded Swiss cheese	250 mL
1/4 cup	minced green onion	50 mL
1/4 cup	chopped red pepper	50 mL
1/4 cup	chopped green pepper	50 mL
4	eggs	4
1 1/2 cups	table cream or evaporated milk, undiluted	375 mL
1/4 tsp	ground nutmeg	1 mL
1/4 tsp	dry mustard	1 mL
	salt and pepper, to taste	

- Preheat oven to 350°F (180°C). In pie shell, spread bacon, cheese, green onion, and red and green peppers.
- In a bowl, beat eggs and combine with cream, nutmeg, mustard, salt and pepper.
- Pour egg mixture over the pie crust.
- Bake 35 to 40 minutes or until a knife inserted near the center comes out clean. Let stand 5 to 10 minutes before cutting into wedges to serve.

Nutrients per serving
Calories: 268
Protein: 6.7 g
Carbohydrate: 13.1 g
Fat: 21.0 g

1

In pie shell, spread filling ingredients.

2

Beat eggs and combine with cream and seasonings.

3

Pour egg mixture over the pie crust.

1

Beat yolks well and add ¼ cup (50 mL) of the warm sauce mixture to them.

2

Fold some of the egg whites into the sauce to make it lighter.

3

Carefully pour into a 4-cup (1 L) soufflé dish or casserole. Bake 20 to 25 minutes or until done.

Soufflé

Makes 4 servings
Preparation: 10 minutes
Cooking: 28 minutes

2 tbsp	butter	30 mL
2 tbsp	all-purpose flour	30 mL
1/2 tsp	salt	2 mL
	pinch ground pepper	
3/4 cup	milk	175 mL
4	egg yolks	4
6	egg whites	6
1/4 tsp	cream of tartar	1 mL

- Preheat oven to 375°F (190°C). In a medium saucepan, melt butter over low heat. Stir in flour, salt and pepper. Cook, stirring constantly, until mixture is smooth and bubbly.

- Stir in milk all at once. Continue stirring until mixture boils and is smooth and thickened.

- In a bowl, beat yolks well and add 1/4 cup (50 mL) of the warm sauce mixture to them. Combine yolk mixture with remaining sauce, blending thoroughly. If desired, add finely chopped filling ingredients and seasoning, stirring into the sauce until well blended (see Variations). Set sauce aside to cool slightly.

- In a large bowl, beat egg whites and cream of tartar until stiff but not dry. Fold about a quarter of the egg whites into the sauce to make it lighter, then gently but thoroughly fold the sauce into the remaining egg whites.

- Carefully pour into a 4-cup (1 L) soufflé dish or casserole. Bake 20 to 25 minutes or until done. Serve immediately.

TIPS: Never add egg yolks to a hot sauce all at once as they may begin to coagulate too rapidly and form lumps.

A small funnel is handy for separating egg whites from yolks. Place the funnel over a measuring cup. Crack the egg over the funnel. The white will run through and the yolk will remain in the funnel.

Variations: Cheese Soufflé – Stir 1 cup (250 mL) grated Swiss cheese and 2 tbsp (30 mL) chopped green onion into sauce mixture.

Crab Soufflé – Stir 1 6-oz (170 g) can salad crab meat, drained, 1/2 tsp (2 mL) each dried thyme and curry powder, and 1/4 tsp (1 mL) garlic salt into sauce mixture.

Vegetable Soufflé – Stir 1 cup (250 mL) cooked, shredded carrot, 1/2 cup (125 mL) grated Cheddar cheese and 1/4 tsp (1 mL) dried dill into sauce mixture.

Nutrients per serving
Calories: 171
Protein: 9.9 g
Carbohydrate: 5.9 g
Fat: 11.7 g

French Toast

Makes 4 pieces
Preparation: 8 minutes
Cooking: 17 minutes

2	eggs	2
1/2 cup	milk	125 mL
1/4 tsp	salt	1 mL
1 tbsp	butter or margarine	15 mL
4	bread slices	4

Nutrients per piece
Calories: 153
Protein: 6.6 g
Carbohydrate: 15.9 g
Fat: 6.8 g

- In a shallow bowl, mix together eggs, milk and salt. Melt butter in a large skillet over medium heat.

- Dip one slice of bread at a time into egg mixture and let soak for 10 seconds on each side.

- Fry soaked bread 1 1/2 to 2 minutes on each side or until golden brown. Add more butter if necessary to keep slices from sticking.

- Transfer French toast to baking sheet and keep warm in oven while cooking remaining bread. Serve with jam, maple syrup, honey or fresh seasonal fruit.

Fried Eggs

Makes 1 serving
Preparation: 1 minute
Cooking: 2 to 3 minutes

2	eggs	2
1 tbsp	butter or margarine	15 mL
	salt and pepper	

- Melt butter in a skillet over medium heat.
- One at a time, break eggs into a small bowl, then slide into skillet.
- Cook slowly to desired doneness.
- Place eggs right-side up on plate. Season with salt and pepper and serve immediately.

Nutrients per serving
Calories: 216
Protein: 12.4 g
Carbohydrate: 1.2 g
Fat: 17.6 g

TIPS: For "sunny-side up" eggs, cook just until whites are set.

For "over easy" eggs, cook until whites are set. Turn over and cook just long enough for a white film to form over yolks, about 30 seconds.

For "over well" eggs, turn eggs over and cook until eggs are completely set, about 1 minute.

For "well done" or "steam-fried eggs", prepare sunny-side up eggs. Cover skillet during last minute of cooking, or spoon 1 tsp (5 mL) water over each egg and cover pan. Cook to desired doneness.

Variation: To make a fried egg in an amusing shape, spray the inside of two 3-inch (7.5 cm) diameter cookie cutters with cooking spray and place in a moderately hot nonstick skillet. Melt 1 tsp (5 mL) butter in the center of each and break an egg into each cookie cutter. Season with salt and pepper. Cook over low heat until eggs are set, using the steam-fried egg method. Loosen eggs from cookie cutters using a small knife and remove eggs. Serve immediately.

Hard Meringues

Hard meringues can be shaped into shells, pie crusts, baskets and all kinds of fancy or plain designs to be filled with ice cream, custards or fresh fruit.

Makes 8 large meringues
Preparation: 15 minutes
Cooking: 45 minutes

6	egg whites, at room temperature	6
1/8 tsp	cream of tartar	0.5 mL
2 cups	sugar	500 mL
1 tsp	vanilla extract	5 mL
1 tbsp	white vinegar	15 mL

- Preheat oven to 275°F (140°C). Grease 2 baking sheets.

- In a large mixing bowl, beat egg whites with electric mixer until foamy. Add cream of tartar and continue beating until soft peaks form.

- Gradually add sugar, 2 tbsp (30 mL) at a time, beating constantly until sugar is dissolved. Add vanilla and vinegar and beat until whites are very stiff and shiny, about 10 minutes more.

- Place about 1/2 cup (125 mL) meringue on baking sheet. Using your hands, pull the meringue into a peak. Smooth the sides, and repeat with remaining meringue. Alternatively, pipe meringue onto baking sheet using a pastry bag.

- Bake until meringues are lightly browned, about 45 minutes. Cool completely on wire racks.

Nutrients per meringue
Calories: 207
Protein: 2.6 g
Carbohydrate: 50.2 g
Fat: 0 g

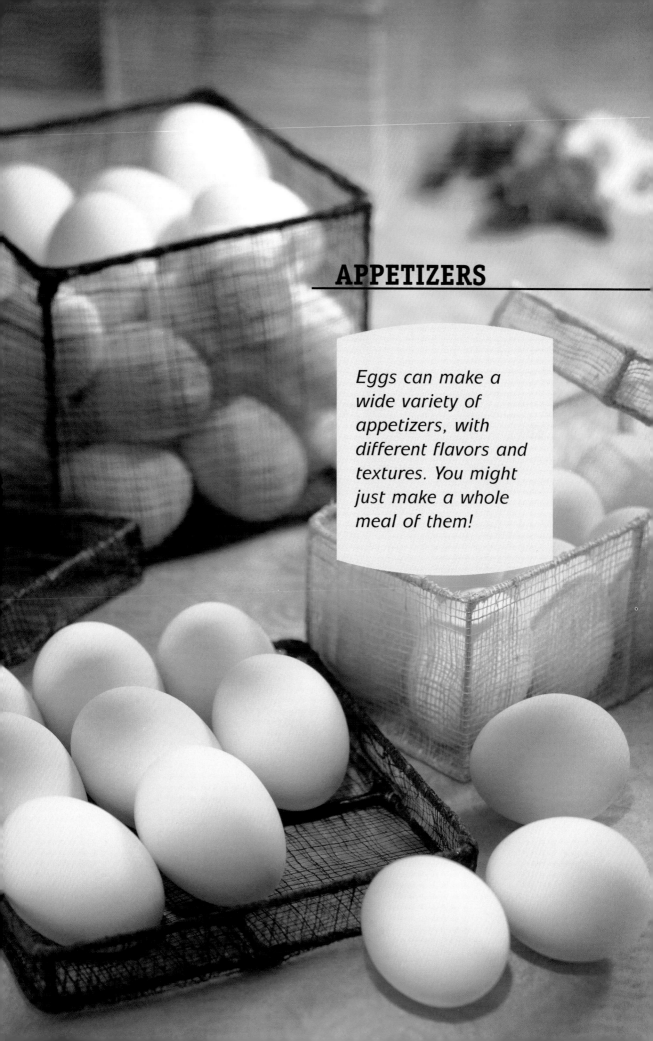

APPETIZERS

Eggs can make a wide variety of appetizers, with different flavors and textures. You might just make a whole meal of them!

Fast Canapés

Makes 24 appetizers
Preparation: 10 minutes

Egg and Caviar Canapés

Combine 1/4 cup (50 mL) mayonnaise
with 1/4 tsp (1 mL) paprika. Spread
1/2 tsp (2 mL) of mixture on each of
24 crackers. Garnish with half a slice of
hard-cooked egg, 1/4 tsp (1 mL) red
caviar and a fresh oregano leaf.

Nutrients per appetizer
Calories: 45
Protein: 1.1 g
Carbohydrate: 3.5 g
Fat: 2.3 g

Variations: Egg Salsa Bites – Spread
crackers with mayonnaise. Garnish with
a thin slice of cucumber, a slice of hard-
cooked egg, and a generous dab of salsa.

Bruschetta Baguette Slices – Toast thin
slices of French baguette. Combine
chopped hard-cooked egg, chopped
tomato, olive oil and chopped fresh basil.
Spread on baguette slices.

Garlic Shrimp and Egg Canapés –
Spread crackers with herb and garlic
Cream cheese dip. Add a slice of hard-
cooked egg, a medium shrimp and a
sprig of parsley.

**Dilled Egg and Smoked Salmon on
Rye** – Combine 1/4 cup (50 mL)
spreadable Cream cheese with 1 tsp
(5 mL) chopped fresh dill. Spread on
thinly sliced rye bread or on crackers.
Garnish with a slice of hard-cooked egg,
a small roll of smoked salmon and fresh
dill or parsley.

Egg & Tomato Bruschetta

Makes 4 appetizers
Preparation: 5 minutes
Cooking: 8 minutes

2¹/₂ cups	diced tomatoes (2 large)	625 mL
¹/₄ cup	chopped fresh basil or 1¹/₂ tsp (7 mL) dried	50 mL
1 tsp	minced garlic	5 mL
	salt and pepper, to taste	
8	thick slices French bread	8
2 tbsp	olive oil	30 mL
4 oz	Cream cheese, softened	125 g
4	hard-cooked eggs, peeled and sliced	4
3 tbsp	freshly grated Parmesan cheese	45 mL
	fresh basil for garnish	

- Place tomatoes in a sieve and let drain over a bowl while preparing remaining ingredients.
- When ready to assemble, combine tomatoes, basil, garlic, salt and pepper in a bowl.

Barbecue Directions

- Preheat barbecue to medium. Brush both sides of bread slices with oil. Place on grill and grill one side only. Remove from grill.

- Spread Cream cheese on toasted side of bread slices. Top each slice with about ¹/₃ cup (75 mL) tomato mixture. Arrange a slice of egg over each. Sprinkle with Parmesan cheese.

- Using a wide metal spatula, place bread on grill. Turn both burners down to low. Close cover and cook for a few minutes or until warmed through, keeping a close watch. If bread browns too quickly underneath, turn the heat off completely. Garnish with fresh basil and serve.

Oven Directions

- Toast bread. Prepare slices as directed above. Bake at 450°F (230°C), 6 to 8 minutes.

Nutrients per appetizer
Calories: 397
Protein: 15.0 g
Carbohydrate: 27.6 g
Fat: 25.5 g

Quick Egg Wedges Giardiniere

Makes 4 servings
Preparation: 10 minutes
Cooking: 15 minutes

1/4 cup	dry breadcrumbs	50 mL
4 tsp	butter, divided	20 mL
6	eggs	6
1/2 cup	milk	125 mL
1/2 tsp	dried basil	2 mL
	salt and pepper, to taste	
2 cups	cooked vegetables	500 mL
1	green onion, chopped	1
1 cup	shredded Cheddar or Swiss cheese	250 mL
	paprika, to taste	

Nutrients per serving
Calories: 327
Protein: 19.9 g
Carbohydrate: 13.1 g
Fat: 21.8 g

- Preheat oven to 375°F (190°C).
- Melt 1 tbsp (15 mL) butter. Combine with breadcrumbs and pat with fingers over bottom and sides of a greased 9-inch (23 cm) pie plate, covering it sparingly. Bake 5 minutes.
- In a bowl, beat together eggs, milk, basil, salt and pepper until just blended. Add cooked vegetables and green onion.
- Melt 1 tsp (5 mL) butter in a large nonstick skillet over medium-high heat. Add egg mixture and cook, stirring constantly with a wide spatula.
- When eggs are almost set but still very moist (about the consistency of soft oatmeal), remove from heat and stir in two-thirds of the cheese. Immediately pour into pie plate. Sprinkle with remaining cheese and paprika.
- Bake 10 to 12 minutes or until eggs are set. Cut into wedges and serve hot or at room temperature.

TIP: For a lunch bag, cool completely. Wrap wedges separately in plastic wrap and refrigerate. To reheat, remove plastic wrap, place one wedge on a paper napkin and reheat in microwave oven on 'High' (100%) 1 to 1 1/2 minutes.

Chicken Roulade Appetizers

Makes 36 appetizers
Preparation: 15 minutes
Cooking: 18 minutes
Refrigeration: 1 hour

Roulade

1/4 cup	butter or margarine	50 mL
1/3 cup	all-purpose flour	75 mL
11/2 cups	milk	375 mL
6	egg yolks	6
1/2 tsp	salt	2 mL
1/4 tsp	ground nutmeg	1 mL
1/4 tsp	pepper	1 mL
6	egg whites	6
1/2 tsp	cream of tartar	2 mL

Filling

11/2 cups	chopped cooked chicken	375 mL
1/2 cup	toasted sliced almonds	125 mL
1/4 cup	chopped fresh parsley	50 mL
2	small green onions, chopped	2
2 tsp	curry powder (optional)	10 mL
1/4 tsp	salt	1 mL
1/2 cup	mayonnaise	125 mL
	cayenne pepper, to taste	

- Preheat oven to 375°F (190°C).
- Lightly grease a 15 x 10-inch (38 x 25 cm) jelly-roll pan or baking sheet with edge. Line with parchment paper or foil, shiny-side up. Grease well and flour lightly.

Roulade

- In a medium saucepan over medium heat, melt butter or margarine. Stir in flour and cook 1 minute. Add milk. Cook, stirring, until mixture comes to a boil; simmer 2 minutes. Remove from heat.
- In a bowl, beat egg yolks, adding a few tablespoons of the hot milk mixture, then beat egg yolk mixture into milk mixture. Season with salt, nutmeg and pepper. Pour into a medium bowl and cool slightly.
- In another bowl, beat egg whites with cream of tartar until stiff but not dry. Gently fold into yolk mixture.
- Spread mixture in prepared pan. Bake 15 to 20 minutes or until golden and top feels firm. Let stand 5 minutes.
- Invert roulade on clean tea towel. Carefully peel off paper in strips. Cool completely. Cut crosswise in half to make 2 rectangles, 10 inches (25 cm) wide.

Filling

- Combine all ingredients. Spread filling on rectangles, leaving a 1-inch (2.5 cm) border on all sides. Starting with 10-inch (25 cm) side, roll up both rectangles. Cover separately with plastic wrap and refrigerate for at least 1 hour. (May be prepared 2 days in advance.) Cut into 1/2-inch (1 cm) slices and serve.

Nutrients per appetizer
Calories: 76
Protein: 3.6 g
Carbohydrate: 1.9 g
Fat: 6.0 g

1

Cut roulade crosswise in half to make 2 rectangles.

2

Spread filling over both rectangles.

3

Roll up both rectangles.

Asparagus Soup

Eggs give a creamy, rich texture to this lemon-flavored soup.

Makes 6 servings
Preparation: 5 minutes
Cooking: 20 minutes

4 cups	chicken stock or broth	1 L
1/3 cup	long grain rice	75 mL
8 oz	fresh asparagus spears, trimmed and sliced diagonally into 1-inch (2.5 cm) pieces	250 g
4	eggs	4
	juice and grated rind of one lemon	
	pepper, to taste	

- In a heavy saucepan, bring stock and rice to a boil. Reduce heat and add asparagus; partially cover and cook 15 minutes or until rice is tender.

- In a small bowl, whisk eggs until well beaten. Stir in lemon juice. Whisk approximately 1 cup (250 mL) hot stock into egg mixture. Slowly add egg mixture to rice mixture, stirring constantly.

- Cook over low heat until smooth and thick. Do not boil or soup will curdle. Remove from heat.

- Stir in lemon rind. Season with pepper.

Nutrients per serving
Calories: 122
Protein: 8.9 g
Carbohydrate: 11.0 g
Fat: 4.4 g

Egg Drop Soup

Makes 4 servings
Preparation: 5 minutes
Cooking: 12 minutes

4 cups	chicken broth	1 L
2 tbsp	soy sauce	30 mL
1	green onion, thinly sliced	1
2	eggs	2

- Combine chicken broth and soy sauce in a 2-quart (2 L) microwaveable bowl. Microwave on 'High' (100%) 10 to 12 minutes or until boiling.
- Stir in green onion.
- In a bowl, beat eggs lightly to blend whites and yolks. Slowly pour eggs into broth in a thin stream, stirring gently.
- Serve immediately.

Nutrients per serving
Calories: 82
Protein: 8.6 g
Carbohydrate: 2.3 g
Fat: 3.9 g

1

Spoon a thin layer of gelatin into mold. Arrange egg slices, green onion and pieces of pepper in a decorative design.

2

Add enough gelatin mixture to cover eggs completely; refrigerate.

3

Pour egg mousse into mold, over clear layer. Refrigerate until firm.

Festive Egg Mousse

Makes 8 servings
Preparation: 30 minutes
Refrigeration: 3 hours
Freezing: 10 minutes

Clear Layer

1/2 cup	*each* canned condensed chicken broth and water	125 mL
1 tbsp	white wine or lemon juice	15 mL
1 1/2 tsp	unflavored gelatin	7 mL
1	hard-cooked egg, peeled and sliced	1
	green onion and peppers, for garnish	

Egg Mousse

1	envelope unflavored gelatin	1
1/2 cup	chicken broth or water	125 mL
5	hard-cooked eggs, peeled	5
1/3 cup	mayonnaise	75 mL
1/4 cup	Cream cheese	50 mL
1 tbsp	Dijon mustard	15 mL
	salt, pepper and hot pepper sauce, to taste	
1/3 cup	*each* chopped green and red peppers	75 mL
1/4 cup	chopped green onion	50 mL

Nutrients per serving
Calories: 165
Protein: 7.8 g
Carbohydrate: 1.9 g
Fat: 14.0 g

Clear Layer

- Strain chicken broth to remove any fat. Combine broth, water and wine in a small bowl. Sprinkle gelatin on top; set over hot water to dissolve.

- Remove bowl from hot water and place in a bowl of water and ice, stirring frequently, until mixture has the consistency of raw egg white. Remove from ice water.

- Spoon a thin layer of gelatin into a greased 5-cup (1.25 L) mold. Arrange egg slices, green onion and pieces of pepper in a decorative design. Place in freezer until set, about 10 minutes. Add enough gelatin mixture to cover eggs completely; refrigerate.

Egg Mousse

- In a small bowl, sprinkle gelatin over chicken broth or water; set over hot water to dissolve.

- In a food processor or blender, purée eggs. Add mayonnaise, Cream cheese, mustard, salt, pepper and hot pepper sauce; purée until well blended. Add dissolved gelatin, green and red peppers and green onion; purée about 1 minute.

- Pour into mold, over clear layer. Refrigerate until firm, at least 3 hours or overnight.

- Remove from mold onto a serving plate. Serve with crackers.

Deviled Eggs with Crab Meat

Makes 12 appetizers
Preparation: 10 minutes

6	hard-cooked eggs, peeled	6
1/4 cup	mayonnaise or salad dressing	50 mL
2 tbsp	finely chopped celery	30 mL
2 tsp	Dijon mustard	10 mL
1 tsp	finely chopped parsley	5 mL
1/8 tsp	oregano	0.5 mL
1/8 tsp	onion powder	0.5 mL
	a few drops Worcestershire sauce	
	salt and pepper, to taste	
1	6-oz (170 g) can salad crab meat, drained	1

- Cut eggs in half lengthwise. Remove yolks and place them in a bowl. Place whites on a platter, cut-side up.
- Mash yolks with a fork; add mayonnaise, celery, mustard, parsley, oregano, onion powder, Worcestershire sauce, salt and pepper. Add crab meat and mix well.
- Refill whites with yolk mixture and garnish as desired. Serve immediately or store covered in refrigerator. Use within 3 days.

TIP: Recipe can be doubled.

Variations: Use finely chopped imitation crab meat, salmon or tuna.

Nutrients per appetizer
Calories: 80
Protein: 4.8 g
Carbohydrate: 0.6 g
Fat: 6.3 g

Chutney Deviled Eggs

This is a sweet, spicy spin on a favorite picnic food.

Makes 8 appetizers
Preparation: 5 minutes

4	hard-cooked eggs, peeled	4
2 tbsp	sour cream	30 mL
1 tbsp	mango chutney, chopped	15 mL
1/4 tsp	curry powder	1 mL
	salt and hot pepper sauce, to taste	
2	green onions, trimmed and minced	2

- Cut eggs in half lengthwise. Remove yolks and place them in a bowl. Place whites on a platter, cut-side up.
- Mash yolks with a fork.
- In a small bowl, mix together sour cream, chutney, curry powder, salt and hot pepper sauce. Add to yolks along with green onions, and mash into a paste.
- Refill whites with yolk mixture and garnish as desired. Serve immediately or store covered in the refrigerator. Use within 3 days.

Nutrients per appetizer
Calories: 49
Protein: 2.4 g
Carbohydrate: 1.9 g
Fat: 3 g

Stracciatella Soup

Makes 6 servings
Preparation: 5 minutes
Cooking: 10 minutes

4	eggs	4
1/3 cup	grated Parmesan cheese	75 mL
2 tbsp	finely chopped fresh parsley	30 mL
	pinch ground nutmeg	
	salt and pepper, to taste	
5 cups	chicken broth	1.25 L

- In a bowl, beat eggs with a fork until they are just blended. Mix in cheese, parsley, nutmeg, salt and pepper.
- In a medium saucepan, bring broth to a boil. Pour in the egg mixture slowly while stirring gently and constantly with a whisk.
- Reduce heat to low. Simmer, still stirring, until eggs are cooked, 2 to 3 minutes.

Nutrients per serving
Calories: 108
Protein: 10.6 g
Carbohydrate: 1.5 g
Fat: 6.1 g

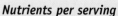

Easy Shrimp Appetizers

*These appetizers are a quick crustless quiche
that can be made a day ahead. Cool
completely, cover with plastic wrap
or foil and keep refrigerated.*

Makes 24 appetizers
Preparation: 15 minutes
Cooking: 25 minutes

4 tsp	butter, divided	20 mL
2 tbsp	dry breadcrumbs	30 mL
6	eggs	6
1/2 cup	milk	125 mL
1/2 tsp	dried basil	2 mL
	salt and pepper, to taste	
	hot pepper sauce, to taste	
1/2 cup	*each* green and red peppers, cut into short strips	125 mL
1/4 cup	chopped onion	50 mL
8 oz	cooked small shrimp, chopped	250 g
1 cup	shredded old Cheddar cheese	250 mL
	paprika, to taste	

- Preheat oven to 375°F (190°C).
- Place 3 tsp (15 mL) butter in a 9-inch (23 cm) square or 11 x 7-inch (27 x 18 cm) baking pan. Melt butter in the oven, about 3 minutes.
- Sprinkle breadcrumbs evenly over melted butter. Bake until browned, 4 to 5 minutes. Set aside.
- In a bowl, beat together eggs, milk, basil, salt, pepper and hot pepper sauce, just until blended. Set aside.
- Melt 1 tsp (5 mL) butter in a large nonstick skillet over medium-high heat. Add green and red peppers and onion. Cook, stirring, 3 minutes. Add egg mixture and shrimp. Cook, stirring constantly with a wide spatula.
- When eggs are almost set but still moist (about the consistency of soft oatmeal), remove from heat and stir in half of the cheese. Immediately pour into baking pan. Sprinkle with remaining cheese and paprika.
- Bake 10 to 12 minutes or until eggs are set. Cool before cutting into squares or bars. Serve warm or at room temperature.

TIP: To serve as a quick quiche, cut into 6 servings. Serve with a salad.

Nutrients per appetizer
Calories: 59
Protein: 5.0 g
Carbohydrate: 1.3 g
Fat: 3.7 g

Primavera Salad

Makes 6 servings
Preparation: 5 minutes
Cooking: 15 minutes
Refrigeration: 1 hour

Salad

3 cups	tri-colored fusilletti	750 mL
1¹/₂ cups	broccoli florets	375 mL
1¹/₂ cups	chopped tomatoes	375 mL
¹/₂ cup	diced green pepper	125 mL
¹/₄ cup	finely chopped green onion	50 mL
6	hard-cooked eggs, peeled and coarsely chopped	6
	pepper, to taste	
	chopped parsley, for garnish	

Dressing

¹/₂ tsp	*each* dry mustard, salt and paprika	2 mL
¹/₄ cup	red wine vinegar	50 mL
¹/₂ cup	vegetable oil	125 mL

- Cook fusilletti according to package directions. Rinse well.

- Cook broccoli in boiling salted water until tender-crisp; drain. Mix with remaining vegetables in a large bowl, and toss with fusilletti.

- Measure mustard, salt and paprika into a small bowl. Add vinegar; stir well. Whisk in oil and pour over salad. Toss well.

- Chill for at least 1 hour before serving. Sprinkle chopped eggs over salad. Season with pepper. Garnish with parsley.

Nutrients per serving
Calories: 440
Protein: 13.5 g
Carbohydrate: 42.2 g
Fat: 24.3 g

Egg Dip with Veggies

Makes 4 servings
Preparation: 15 minutes

4	hard-cooked eggs, peeled	4
1/3 cup	plain yogurt	75 mL
2 tbsp	light mayonnaise	30 mL
2 tbsp	chopped green onion	30 mL
2 tsp	chopped fresh dill or 1/2 tsp (2 mL) dried	10 mL
2 tsp	chopped fresh basil or 1/4 tsp (1 mL) dried	10 mL
1 tsp	Dijon mustard	5 mL
	salt, cayenne pepper and garlic powder, to taste	
	raw vegetables*	
	Swiss or Brick cheese cubes	
	pita bread wedges or bread sticks	

* Such as sweet pepper strips, celery or carrot sticks, cucumber slices, broccoli or cauliflower florets, cherry tomatoes and mushrooms.

- In a food processor or blender, purée eggs.
- Blend in yogurt, mayonnaise, onion, dill, basil and mustard. Season with salt, cayenne pepper and garlic powder.
- Refrigerate, covered, and serve within 3 days with vegetables, cheese and pita bread wedges or bread sticks.

Nutrients per serving
Calories: 114
Protein: 7.2 g
Carbohydrate: 3.0 g
Fat: 7.8 g

French Egg and Potato Salad

Here's a fresher, lighter-tasting potato salad.

Makes 6 servings
Preparation: 10 minutes

6	medium potatoes, peeled, cooked and diced	6
4	hard-cooked eggs, peeled and chopped	4
2	green onions, chopped	2
3 tbsp	vegetable oil	45 mL
3 tbsp	vinegar	45 mL
1 tsp	Dijon mustard	5 mL
1/2 tsp	salt	2 mL
1/4 tsp	pepper	1 mL
	paprika, for garnish	

Nutrients per serving
Calories: 231
Protein: 6.6 g
Carbohydrate: 28.0 g
Fat: 11.0 g

- In a bowl, toss together potatoes, eggs and green onions.
- In a small jar with a lid, shake together oil, vinegar, mustard, salt and pepper.
- Pour vinegar mixture over potatoes; toss gently until well mixed.
- Spoon into serving bowl; sprinkle with paprika. Cover and refrigerate. For best flavor, remove from refrigerator 15 minutes before serving.

Variation: German-Style Egg and Potato Salad – Add 1/2 cup (125 mL) chopped dill pickles and 3 slices cooked, crumbled bacon to potato mixture before adding vinaigrette. Substitute grainy Dijon mustard for the smooth Dijon mustard in vinaigrette.

Waldorf Coleslaw

Makes 10 servings
Preparation: 3 minutes
Refrigeration: 3 hours

6	hard-cooked eggs, peeled and grated	6
6 cups	shredded cabbage	1.5 L
2 cups	chopped apples	500 mL
1/2 cup	raisins	125 mL
1/4 cup	roasted peanuts	50 mL
1/2 cup	mayonnaise	125 mL

- Mix all ingredients together and chill for at least 3 hours before serving.

Nutrients per serving
Calories: 194
Protein: 5.6 g
Carbohydrate: 13.3 g
Fat: 13.8 g

1

Spoon vegetables over
egg layer and sprinkle
with ¼ cup (50 mL)
cheese.

2

Starting with long side,
roll jelly-roll style.

3

Place seam-side down in
shallow baking pan.
Drizzle with remaining
milk. Sprinkle with
remaining cheese.

Veggie Egg Roll-Up

Makes 6 servings
Preparation: 20 minutes
Cooking: 20 minutes

	cooking spray	
1½ cups	sliced fresh mushrooms	375 mL
1	medium zucchini, sliced	1
½	medium red pepper, diced	½
⅓ cup	chopped onion	75 mL
½ tsp	dried basil	2 mL
6	eggs, separated	6
3 tbsp	all-purpose flour	45 mL
¼ tsp	*each* salt and pepper	1 mL
1¼ cups	hot milk	300 mL
½ cup	shredded old Cheddar cheese	125 mL

- Preheat oven to 350°F (180°C). Spray a 15 x 10-inch (38 x 25 cm) jelly-roll pan with cooking spray. Line with waxed paper and spray again.
- Spray a large skillet with cooking spray. Add vegetables and basil; sauté over medium heat until vegetables are tender-crisp. Set aside.
- In a small bowl, beat together egg yolks, flour, salt and pepper until blended.
- In a large bowl, beat egg whites until stiff but not dry. Gently fold yolk mixture into whites. Spread mixture evenly into jelly-roll pan.
- Bake until firm to the touch, about 8 minutes. Invert onto clean waxed paper. Remove pan and peel off paper liner.
- Increase oven temperature to 375°F (190°C). Spoon ¾ cup (175 mL) milk evenly over egg layer. Spoon vegetables on top and sprinkle with ¼ cup (50 mL) cheese. Starting with long side, roll jelly-roll style. Place seam-side down in shallow baking pan. Drizzle with remaining milk. Sprinkle with remaining cheese. Bake 10 to 12 minutes. Cut into 12 slices.

TIP: To prepare ahead, complete roll-up but do not bake. Cover with plastic wrap and refrigerate. Bake 20 to 25 minutes before serving.

Nutrients per serving
Calories: 188
Protein: 11.4 g
Carbohydrate: 10.0 g
Fat: 11.5 g

Greek Spinach Tarts

Makes 18 tarts
Preparation: 5 minutes
Cooking: 25 minutes

4	eggs	4
1/2 cup	plain yogurt	125 mL
1/2 cup	milk	125 mL
1/2 tsp	salt	2 mL
1/4 tsp	dry mustard	1 mL
1/2 tsp	tarragon	2 mL
	dash ground nutmeg	
10 oz	spinach, chopped, cooked and drained	300 g
1/2 cup	crumbled Feta cheese	125 mL
18	medium pastry-lined tart tins	18

- Preheat oven to 375°F (190°F).
- In a bowl, beat eggs until blended and mix in yogurt, milk, salt, mustard, tarragon, nutmeg, spinach and Feta.
- Spoon into pastry-lined tart tins.
- Bake tarts for 25 minutes, until set.

Nutrients per tart
Calories: 136
Protein: 4.0 g
Carbohydrate: 10.2 g
Fat: 8.8 g

BREAKFAST AND BRUNCH

Nothing says "breakfast" or "brunch" like eggs. Here are some great recipes to add to your collection.

Eggs Benedict with Cheddar Sauce

Makes 4 servings
Preparation: 10 minutes
Cooking: 10 minutes

1 cup	milk	250 mL
1 tbsp	cornstarch	15 mL
2 tbsp	butter or margarine	30 mL
	salt, pepper and ground nutmeg, to taste	
1 cup	shredded Cheddar cheese	250 mL
8	eggs	8
4	English muffins, split and toasted	4
8	thin slices Orange-Glazed Ham*	8
	shredded Cheddar cheese and chopped fresh parsley, for garnish	

*Orange-Glazed Ham – For flavorful baked ham, brush the following orange glaze on ham during the last half-hour of baking (bake uncovered): In a small bowl, stir together 1/2 cup (125 mL) corn syrup, 2 tbsp (30 mL) each orange juice and slivered orange rind and 1/4 tsp (1 mL) each ground cinnamon and ginger. *Makes 3/4 cup (175 mL)*.

- In a small saucepan, gradually stir milk into cornstarch until smooth. Add butter, salt, pepper and nutmeg. Stirring constantly, bring to boil over medium heat; boil 1 minute to thicken. Add cheese and stir until smooth. Keep hot.
- Poach eggs as directed on page 16.
- Place two muffin halves on each of 4 dinner plates. Top each muffin half with a slice of ham, a poached egg and 2 tbsp (30 mL) cheese sauce. Garnish with shredded cheese and parsley. Serve immediately.

Variations: Quick Microwave Hollandaise Sauce – In a 4-cup (1 L) microwaveable bowl, soften 1/2 cup (125 mL) butter in microwave on 'High' (100%) for 5 to 10 seconds. Add 3 egg yolks, whisking until smooth. Microwave for four 15-second intervals on 'High' (100%), stirring sauce after each heating. Whisk in 1 tbsp (15 mL) lemon juice and a pinch of cayenne pepper. Use immediately.

Yogurt Hollandaise Sauce – In top of double boiler, whisk together 3/4 cup (175 mL) plain yogurt, 2 eggs, 2 tsp (10 mL) sugar, 1/4 tsp (1 mL) salt, 1/2 tsp (2 mL) grated lemon rind and 1/4 tsp (1 mL) hot pepper sauce. Cook over simmering water, stirring constantly, 10 to 12 minutes.

Nutrients per serving
Calories: 559
Protein: 34.5 g
Carbohydrate: 34.0 g
Fat: 30.9 g

Poached Eggs Primavera

Makes 4 servings
Preparation: 15 minutes
Cooking: 18 minutes

Lemon Parsley Sauce

2 tbsp	butter or margarine	30 mL
2 1/2 tbsp	all-purpose flour	40 mL
1 cup	chicken broth	250 mL
2 tbsp	whipping cream (optional)	30 mL
2 tbsp	chopped fresh parsley	30 mL
2 tsp	lemon juice	10 mL
	salt and pepper, to taste	
1 lb	fresh asparagus, trimmed (or a 10-oz (300 g) package of frozen asparagus spears)	500 g
4	slices cooked ham	4
8	slices bread	8
8	eggs	8

- To prepare sauce, melt butter or margarine in a small saucepan over medium heat. Stir in flour and cook 1 minute. Add chicken broth. Cook, stirring, until mixture comes to a boil. Reduce heat and simmer 2 minutes. Remove from heat. Stir in cream (if using), parsley, lemon juice, salt and pepper. Keep hot or reheat before serving.

- Cook fresh asparagus in a small amount of water until tender crisp (or cook frozen asparagus as directed on package). Drain. Divide into 4 bundles and wrap each bundle with a slice of ham. Reheat in microwave oven on 'High' (100%) 1 1/2 to 2 minutes before serving.

- With a 4-inch (10 cm) cutter, make decorative cut-outs in bread slices; toast when ready to serve.

- Just before serving, poach eggs (as described on page 16).

- To serve, place a ham and asparagus bundle on each of 4 warmed dinner plates. Alongside, serve 2 eggs on toasted bread cut-outs and spoon sauce over top.

Nutrients per serving
Calories: 413
Protein: 25.0 g
Carbohydrate: 30.9 g
Fat: 20.8 g

1

Divide asparagus into 4 bundles and wrap each bundle with a slice of ham.

2

With a 4-inch (10 cm) cutter, make decorative cut-outs in bread slices.

3

Serve a ham and asparagus bundle on each plate. Alongside, serve 2 eggs on toasted bread cut-outs and spoon sauce over top.

Poached Eggs with Vegetables

Makes 4 servings
Preparation: 10 minutes
Cooking: 12 minutes

8	eggs	8
2 cups	seasoned cooked vegetables*	500 mL
	salt and pepper, to taste	
2 tbsp	grated Parmesan cheese	30 mL
4	crusty rolls	4

*Use mixed fresh or frozen vegetables or ratatouille.

- Poach eggs as described on page 16. Remove with slotted spoon; drain on paper towels 1 minute. Transfer eggs to a plate.

- Divide vegetables among 4 microwaveable containers, building an edge all around. Place 2 poached eggs in the middle of each container.

- Season with salt and pepper. Sprinkle Parmesan cheese on top.

- Microwave on 'High' (100%) until hot, 1 to 1 1/2 minutes. Serve with a crusty roll.

Nutrients per serving
Calories: 412
Protein: 22.5 g
Carbohydrate: 50.4 g
Fat: 13.1 g

Egg-Stuffed Ham Rolls

Makes 4 servings
Preparation: 10 minutes
Cooking: 8 minutes

8	eggs	8
1/3 cup	table cream	75 mL
2 tbsp	finely chopped fresh parsley	30 mL
1/2 tsp	seasoned salt	2 mL
1/2 tsp	fine herbs	2 mL
1/8 tsp	pepper	0.5 mL
3 tbsp	butter or margarine	45 mL
4 oz	Cream cheese, cut into small pieces	125 g
8	thin slices cooked ham, round (6-inch/15 cm diameter) or rectangular	8
	green onion or tomato slices and parsley, for garnish	

- In a bowl, whisk together eggs, cream, parsley, seasoned salt, fine herbs and pepper.
- In a large skillet, melt butter. Pour egg mixture into skillet and scramble over medium-low heat until just set. Stir Cream cheese into eggs. Remove from heat.
- Lay ham slices flat. Spoon about 1/4 cup (50 mL) egg mixture onto each slice, then roll them up.
- Place on serving platter. Garnish with green onion or tomato slices and parsley.

TIP: Tie the top part of a green onion around each roll to make a bundle.

Nutrients per serving
Calories: 425
Protein: 23.3 g
Carbohydrate: 3.5 g
Fat: 35.1 g

Creamy Fettuccine

Makes 4 servings
Preparation: 10 minutes
Cooking: 15 minutes

5	eggs	5
3/4 cup	grated Parmesan cheese	175 mL
2 tbsp	finely chopped fresh parsley	30 mL
12 oz	uncooked fettuccine	350 g
2 tbsp	butter	30 mL
2	garlic cloves, minced	2
8 oz	fresh mushrooms, sliced	250 g
1/2 cup	10% cream	125 mL
	salt and freshly ground pepper, to taste	

- In a bowl, beat together eggs, Parmesan cheese and parsley until eggs are just blended.

- Cook fettuccine al dente, in boiling salted water. (Do not cook ahead.)

- Meanwhile, heat a large skillet over medium-high heat. Add butter. When melted, add garlic and mushrooms. Sauté until golden brown, about 3 minutes.

- Add cream, then heat without boiling.

- In a colander, drain pasta but do not rinse. Return to cooking pot immediately.

- Add both mushroom-cream mixture and egg-cheese mixture to the pasta. Toss until eggs thicken and coat fettuccine, 1 to 2 minutes. Season with salt and pepper. Serve immediately.

Nutrients per serving
Calories: 594
Protein: 28.2 g
Carbohydrate: 68.8 g
Fat: 22.4 g

Saucy Salmon Loaf

Makes 5 servings
Preparation: 15 minutes
Cooking: 35 minutes

1	15-oz (426 g) can pink salmon, drained (reserve broth)	1
2 cups	soft breadcrumbs (about 3 slices)	500 mL
1/4 cup	finely chopped onion	50 mL
1/3 cup	chopped fresh parsley	75 mL
3/4 tsp	dried tarragon or savory	3 mL
3	eggs	3
1/4 tsp	*each* salt and pepper	1 mL
3/4 cup	hot liquid (salmon broth and milk)	175 mL

Cheese Sauce

2 tbsp	butter	30 mL
2 tbsp	all-purpose flour	30 mL
	salt, dry mustard and cayenne pepper, to taste	
1¼ cups	milk	300 mL
1/2 cup	shredded Cheddar or Swiss cheese	125 mL

- Preheat oven to 350°F (180°C).
- In a large bowl, flake salmon with a fork, crushing skin and bones. Add breadcrumbs, onion, parsley and tarragon or savory. Mix well.
- Place mixture in well-greased nonstick 9 x 5-inch (23 x 13 cm) loaf pan.
- In a bowl, beat together eggs, salt and pepper until eggs are just blended. Stir in hot liquid. Pour over salmon mixture in loaf pan.
- Bake 30 to 35 minutes or until firm. Loosen loaf with a spatula and turn out of pan.
- Meanwhile, make cheese sauce. In a small saucepan, melt butter over medium heat. Stir in flour and seasonings. Stir in milk. Cook, stirring constantly, until sauce thickens and comes to a boil. Cook 1 minute longer. Remove from heat. Add cheese and stir until smooth. Serve with salmon loaf.

Nutrients per serving
Calories: 351
Protein: 28 g
Carbohydrate: 16.5 g
Fat: 18.6 g

Tuna & Noodle Bake

Makes 4 servings
Preparation: 15 minutes
Cooking: 40 minutes

2¹/₂ cups	medium or broad egg noodles	625 mL
1	10-oz (300 g) package frozen chopped spinach, thawed and squeezed dry	1
1	6¹/₂-oz (184 g) can chunk light tuna, drained* (reserve broth)	1
2	green onions, chopped	2
1¹/₂ cups	shredded Gouda or Swiss cheese	375 mL
4	eggs	4
1 cup	liquid (tuna broth and milk)	250 mL
	salt and cayenne pepper, to taste	

* Or 1 7¹/₂-oz (212 g) can salmon, drained and flaked

- Preheat oven to 350°F (180°C)
- Cook noodles in boiling salted water. Drain and set aside.
- In a large bowl, combine noodles, spinach, tuna, green onions and 1 cup (250 mL) cheese. Spoon mixture into well-greased deep 9-inch (23 cm) pie plate.
- In a medium-size microwaveable bowl, beat together eggs, liquid, salt and cayenne pepper until eggs are just blended. Microwave on 'High' (100%), stirring often, until mixture thickens slightly.
- Pour over noodle and tuna mixture. Sprinkle with remaining cheese. Bake 35 to 40 minutes or until cheese is golden.

Nutrients per serving
Calories: 399
Protein: 32.6 g
Carbohydrate: 23.6 g
Fat: 19.1 g

Egg, Tomato and Cheese Salad

Makes 4 servings
Preparation: 10 minutes

4 cups	torn salad greens	1 L
4	hard-cooked eggs, peeled and sliced	4
3 oz	cubed Mozzarella cheese (or 4 slices processed Mozzarella cheese)	90 g
4	tomatoes, sliced	4
	black olives (optional)	
1/3 cup	herb vinaigrette	75 mL

- Divide salad greens among 4 dinner plates.
- Arrange eggs, cheese and tomato slices on top of lettuce.
- Garnish with black olives. Drizzle vinaigrette over top. Serve immediately.

TIP: For a picnic, place salad ingredients in a plastic container with a cover. Pack vinaigrette separately.

Nutrients per serving
Calories: 272
Protein: 12.7 g
Carbohydrate: 9.7 g
Fat: 20.9 g

Egg & Tomato Pasta Salad

Makes 6 servings
Preparation: 15 minutes
Refrigeration: 1 hour

5 cups	medium farfalle, bows or spiral-shaped pasta	1.25 L
1/2 cup	sun-dried tomatoes	125 mL
1/2 cup	*each* diced green, red and yellow peppers	125 mL
1/2 cup	chopped onion or green onion	125 mL
2 tbsp	chopped fresh parsley or basil	30 mL
5	hard-cooked eggs, peeled and chopped	5
1/2 cup	cherry tomatoes, halved (optional)	125 mL

Vinaigrette

1/2 cup	corn oil	125 mL
1/4 cup	red wine vinegar	50 mL
1	garlic clove, minced	1
	salt and pepper, to taste	

- Cook pasta according to package directions. Rinse under cold water. Drain thoroughly and place in a large bowl.

- If using dry-packed tomatoes, soak in hot water 1 minute; drain and pat dry. Chop tomatoes coarsely; add to pasta. Add peppers, onion and parsley.

- To make vinaigrette, combine ingredients in a screw-top jar. Shake well.

- Toss pasta mixture with 1/4 cup (50 mL) vinaigrette. Add eggs and toss carefully. Cover tightly; refrigerate both salad and remaining vinaigrette at least 1 hour.

- Just before serving, add cherry tomatoes to salad; toss salad with remaining vinaigrette. Adjust seasoning to taste.

Nutrients per serving
Calories: 509
Protein: 15.0 g
Carbohydrate: 58.6 g
Fat: 23.8 g

Cheesy Lasagna Roll-Ups

A light and fresh-tasting lasagna that can be in the oven in minutes.

Makes 4 servings
Preparation: 15 minutes
Cooking: 40 minutes
(In microwave: 10 minutes)

8	oven-ready lasagna noodles	8

Sauce

1 tsp	vegetable oil	5 mL
6	mushrooms, sliced	6
1	garlic clove, minced	1
1	19-oz (540 mL) can tomatoes, undrained	1
1 tsp	dried thyme	5 mL

Filling

1	egg, beaten	1
3	hard-cooked eggs, peeled and chopped	3
3/4 cup	Cottage cheese	175 mL
1/2 cup	shredded part-skim Mozzarella cheese	125 mL
1/4 cup	grated Parmesan cheese	50 mL
2 tbsp	chopped parsley	30 mL

- Place noodles in an 11 x 7-inch (28 x 18 cm) baking dish; cover with boiling water and let stand about 8 minutes or until soft. Drain and spread on flat surface.
- Preheat oven to 350°F (180°C).
- Heat oil in a skillet over medium heat. Sauté mushrooms and garlic 3 minutes, or until soft.
- Add tomatoes and thyme. Simmer 10 minutes to thicken.
- Mix the filling ingredients together in a bowl.
- Divide filling evenly among the 8 noodles and spread along the length of each noodle. Roll up noodles and place in baking dish.
- Pour sauce over noodles and cover.
- Bake 40 minutes, or until filling is set. Let stand 5 minutes before serving.

Microwave Method

- Prepare rolls as directed above and place in microwaveable dish. Pour sauce over rolls, cover and cook in microwave oven on 'Medium-high' (70%) for 10 minutes, or until filling is set.

Variation: Spread 1 cup (250 mL) chopped, cooked and drained spinach on top of egg mixture before rolling.

Nutrients per serving
Calories: 370
Protein: 25.0 g
Carbohydrate: 40.0 g
Fat: 12.0 g

1

Bring broth to a boil.
Stirring constantly, slowly
add eggs in a steady
stream. Continue to stir
and cook 1 minute, or
just until eggs are set.

2

Remove from heat.
Stir in couscous; cover
and let stand 5 minutes.

3

Stir in chopped
vegetables, green onion
and cilantro.

Tabbouli Egg Salad

Makes 4 servings
Preparation: 15 minutes
Cooking: 5 minutes

1 cup	chicken or vegetable broth	250 mL
4	eggs, lightly beaten	4
1 cup	couscous or instant rice	250 mL
2 cups	chopped mixed fresh vegetables (e.g., tomato, cucumber, carrot)	500 mL
1	green onion, chopped	1
2 tbsp	chopped fresh cilantro (coriander), mint or parsley	30 mL
1/2 cup	fat-free Italian salad dressing	125 mL
3 tbsp	lemon or lime juice	45 mL
1 tsp	chili powder	5 mL
	salt and pepper, to taste	

- In a large saucepan, bring broth to a boil. Stirring constantly, slowly add eggs in a steady stream. Continue to stir and cook 1 minute, or just until eggs are set.
- Remove from heat. Stir in couscous; cover and let stand 5 minutes.
- Stir in chopped vegetables, green onion and cilantro.
- Combine salad dressing, lemon juice and chili powder. Toss with couscous until well combined. Season with salt and pepper. Refrigerate covered.

Nutrients per serving
Calories: 289
Protein: 14.2 g
Carbohydrate: 44.4 g
Fat: 5.9 g

Breakfast in a Jiffy

Makes 1 serving
Preparation: 5 minutes
Cooking: 3 minutes

2	eggs	2
2 tbsp	milk	30 mL
	pinch dried basil or Italian seasoning	
	salt and pepper, to taste	
2 tbsp	shredded Cheddar cheese	30 mL
1/2 tsp	chopped parsley (optional)	2 mL

Nutrients per serving
Calories: 221
Protein: 17.0 g
Carbohydrate: 2.9 g
Fat: 15.2 g

- In a microwaveable mug, beat together eggs, milk and seasonings.
- Cover loosely with plastic wrap, leaving a small vent.
- Microwave on 'Medium-high' (70%) 1 to 1 1/2 minutes.
- Remove plastic wrap and stir. Sprinkle with cheese and parsley; cover and let stand 1 minute.

TIP: For a breakfast on the go, cut a whole wheat pita bread in half and spoon egg mixture into both pockets.

Variations: After beating eggs, add any of the following: chopped green onion, chopped green, red or yellow pepper, or chopped cooked vegetables or meat. Substitute shredded Mozzarella, Monterey Jack, Colby or Swiss cheese for Cheddar cheese.

Turkey Burger Melts

Makes 4 servings
Preparation: 5 minutes
Cooking: 15 minutes

1	egg	1
2 tbsp	Dijon mustard	30 mL
1/2 tsp	dried tarragon	2 mL
1/4 tsp	*each* salt and pepper	1 mL
1 lb	ground turkey (or chicken)	500 g
1/4 cup	chopped green onion	50 mL
3 tbsp	dry breadcrumbs	45 mL
1 tbsp	vegetable oil	15 mL
1 cup	shredded Swiss cheese (or 4 slices processed Swiss cheese)	250 mL

Nutrients per serving
Calories: 355
Protein: 30.7 g
Carbohydrate: 5.8 g
Fat: 22.7 g

- In a large bowl, beat egg with mustard, tarragon, salt and pepper until blended.
- Add turkey, green onion and breadcrumbs. Mix well.
- Shape mixture into 4 patties, about 1/2-inch (1 cm) thick.
- In a medium nonstick skillet, heat oil over medium heat. Cook patties 5 to 7 minutes on each side, or until turkey is no longer pink.
- Remove skillet from heat. Top each patty with cheese. Cover and let stand until cheese is melted, about 2 minutes.

Variation: Burgers On Buns – Serve patties on toasted kaiser rolls. Garnish with lettuce and sliced tomato.

Sunny Egg Muffins

Makes 4 servings
Preparation: 5 minutes
Cooking: 5 minutes

4	slices back bacon, cooked ham or turkey	4
1 tbsp	butter	15 mL
4	eggs	4
	salt and pepper, to taste	
4	whole wheat English muffins, split and toasted	4
4	slices Colby or processed cheese	4

- Place bacon slices in single layer on a dinner plate. Cover with waxed paper.
- Microwave on 'High' (100%) 2 to 2½ minutes, rotating plate after 1 minute.
- Melt butter in a skillet over medium heat. Break eggs into skillet. With a spatula, break each yolk and mix a bit with the white. Season with salt and pepper.
- When eggs are set, turn and cook briefly on the other side.
- Place each cooked egg on a toasted muffin half. Top with a slice of bacon, ham or turkey and a slice of cheese. Cover with the other toasted muffin half.

Nutrients per serving
Calories: 401
Protein: 24.7 g
Carbohydrate: 28.9 g
Fat: 21.4 g

Blueberry Muffins *à la Suisse*

Makes 12 large muffins
Preparation: 10 minutes
Baking: 25 minutes

2 cups	whole wheat or all-purpose flour	500 mL
2/3 cup	brown sugar, packed	150 mL
1 tbsp	baking powder	15 mL
1/2 tsp	salt	2 mL
1 tbsp	grated orange rind	15 mL
1½ cups	shredded Swiss cheese	375 mL
1½ cups	fresh or frozen blueberries	375 mL
2	eggs	2
1 cup	milk	250 mL
1/4 cup	melted butter	50 mL
1 tsp	vanilla extract	5 mL

Nutrients per serving
Calories: 236
Protein: 8.6 g
Carbohydrate: 30.9 g
Fat: 9.4 g

- Preheat oven to 375°F (190°C).
- In a large bowl, combine flour, brown sugar, baking powder, salt and orange rind. Mix well. Stir in cheese and blueberries.
- In another bowl, beat together eggs, milk, butter and vanilla. Pour over dry ingredients and stir just until moistened.
- Spoon into large greased or paper-lined muffin tins, filling them three-quarters full. Bake 20 to 25 minutes, or until golden brown and firm to the touch.
- Let stand 5 minutes before turning out onto rack. Serve warm or cold.

TIP: Make these muffins ahead; they freeze well. To reheat, wrap a muffin in a paper towel and microwave at 'Defrost' until warm, about 2 minutes.

1

Arrange bread slices to fit in single layer in dish.

2

Sprinkle with cinnamon.

3

Pour eggs beaten with milk, syrup, butter and vanilla evenly over bread and bake.

Baked Cinnamon French Toast

Makes 6 servings
Preparation: 10 minutes
Cooking: 30 minutes

	cooking spray	
6	bread slices (white, whole grain or raisin)	6
1 tsp	ground cinnamon	5 mL
3	eggs	3
1/2 cup	milk	125 mL
1/2 cup	maple or table syrup	125 mL
2 tbsp	butter or margarine, melted	30 mL
1 tsp	vanilla extract	5 mL
	fruit, for garnish (optional)	
	maple or table syrup	

- Preheat oven to 350°F (180°C).
- Spray a 13 x 9-inch (33 x 23 cm) baking dish with cooking spray. Arrange bread slices to fit in a single layer in dish; sprinkle with cinnamon.
- In a bowl, beat eggs with milk, syrup, butter and vanilla just until blended. Pour evenly over bread.
- Bake uncovered for 30 minutes, or until firm to the touch. Garnish with fruit. Serve hot, with additional syrup.

TIPS: It is important to arrange bread slices in a single layer. If recipe is increased, use another baking dish.

You can bake French toast immediately, or cover and refrigerate several hours or overnight.

Nutrients per serving
Calories: 231
Protein: 6.3 g
Carbohydrate: 32.6 g
Fat: 8.4 g

French Toast with Cheese

Makes 4 servings
Preparation: 10 minutes
Cooking: 5 minutes

8	slices French bread, about 1/2-inch (1 cm) thick, preferably stale	8
4 oz	Cream cheese, softened	125 g
1/2 cup	raspberry jam	125 mL
4	eggs	4
1/2 cup	milk	125 mL
1/2 tsp	vanilla extract	2 mL
1 tbsp	vegetable oil	15 mL
	icing sugar	

Nutrients per serving
Calories: 485
Protein: 14.4 g
Carbohydrate: 58.7 g
Fat: 21.4 g

- Spread Cream cheese evenly on 4 slices of bread. Spread jam over cheese. Top with remaining slices of bread.

- Beat together eggs, milk and vanilla in a shallow dish just large enough to hold the four sandwiches.

- Place sandwiches in dish and soak each side with egg mixture.

- In a nonstick skillet, heat oil over medium-low heat. Fry sandwiches until golden brown, 2 1/2 to 3 minutes per side. Sprinkle with icing sugar and serve.

Variation: Ham and Cheese Toast – Substitute slices of cooked ham and Swiss cheese for the Cream cheese and jam.

Maple Syrup Fried Eggs

Makes 1 serving
Preparation: 5 minutes
Cooking: 7 minutes

2 tbsp	maple syrup	30 mL
2	eggs	2
2	frozen waffles	2

- In a nonstick skillet, heat maple syrup over medium heat.
- Break eggs into maple syrup.
- While eggs are cooking, toast waffles.
- When eggs are cooked to desired doneness, place on waffles, pouring hot maple syrup over top. Serve immediately.

Nutrients per serving
Calories: 501
Protein: 17.5 g
Carbohydrate: 60.3 g
Fat: 21.0 g

Festive Brunch Pie

Makes 10 servings
Preparation: 20 minutes
Cooking: 50 minutes

1	10-oz (300 g) package frozen chopped spinach, thawed	1
3	eggs, slightly beaten	3
1½ cups	Ricotta cheese	375 mL
1 cup	shredded Fontina or Mozzarella cheese	250 mL
½ cup	freshly grated Parmesan cheese	125 mL
¼ cup	finely chopped onion	50 mL
¼ cup	finely chopped fresh parsley	50 mL
	salt, pepper and ground nutmeg, to taste	
	cooking spray	
	pastry for a double-crust pie	
4 tsp	mustard, divided	20 mL
6 oz	sliced cooked ham (or turkey or Italian salami)	175 g
6	hard-cooked eggs, peeled and sliced	6
1	egg, lightly beaten	1

Nutrients per serving
Calories: 473
Protein: 22.5 g
Carbohydrate: 23.1 g
Fat: 38.1 g

- Preheat oven to 400°F (200°C).

- Press spinach to remove excess moisture. Combine eggs, cheeses, spinach, onion, parsley, salt, pepper and nutmeg. Mix thoroughly.

- Lightly spray a 9 x 5-inch (23 x 13 cm) loaf pan with cooking spray.

- On a lightly floured surface, roll out two-thirds of pastry into a 16 x 11-inch (40 x 27 cm) rectangle. Ease pastry into pan. Brush with 2 tsp (10 mL) mustard.

- Layer ingredients in pan, as follows: half of ham, half of cheese mixture, sliced eggs, remaining ham and remaining cheese mixture. Brush top of cheese mixture with remaining 2 tsp (10 mL) mustard. Trim pastry even with pan; brush edge with beaten egg.

- Roll out remaining pastry into an 11 x 7-inch (27 x 17 cm) rectangle. Place over loaf. Trim excess dough to ½ inch (1 cm) all around. Fold excess dough under bottom crust and seal. Brush top with beaten egg. Make slits on top with a sharp knife.

- Bake pie in lower third of oven 50 to 60 minutes, or until pastry is golden brown.

- Remove from oven and cool 30 minutes on wire rack. Loosen sides with a spatula and turn out on rack. Turn right-side up and serve.

SANDWICHES AND SNACKS

There is more to egg sandwiches than egg salad! This chapter will introduce you to a variety of wonderful ways to put eggs and bread together, along with some great snack ideas.

Three-Star Bagels

Makes 4 servings
Preparation: 10 minutes

4 oz	regular or spreadable Cream cheese, softened	125 g
2 tbsp	chopped green onion	30 mL
4	hard-cooked eggs, peeled and coarsely chopped	4
1	3.5-oz (106 g) can salmon, drained	1
	salt and pepper, to taste	
4	bagels, cut in half	4
	lettuce leaves	

- In a bowl, combine Cream cheese and onion. Stir in eggs and salmon. Season with salt and pepper.
- Spread filling on bagel halves.
- Garnish with lettuce. Serve immediately.

TIP: Before garnishing the bagels with lettuce, you can cover them with plastic wrap and refrigerate.

Nutrients per serving
Calories: 468
Protein: 21.6 g
Carbohydrate: 51.4 g
Fat: 18.8 g

Sliced-Egg Sandwich

Makes 1 serving
Preparation: 10 minutes

Honey-Mustard Dressing

1/3 cup	mayonnaise	75 mL
2 tbsp	plain yogurt	30 mL
2 tsp	Dijon mustard	10 mL
2 tsp	honey	10 mL

1	whole grain bun or kaiser roll	1
4	fresh basil leaves (optional)	4
2	hard-cooked eggs, peeled and sliced	2
1	small tomato, sliced	1
6	thin cucumber slices	6
	alfalfa sprouts, watercress or lettuce leaves	

- To make dressing, combine mayonnaise, yogurt, mustard and honey in a small bowl.
- Split bun or roll in half.
- If using basil leaves, place them on bottom half of bun. Arrange egg, tomato and cucumber slices on top of basil and drizzle with 2 tbsp (30 mL) dressing.
- Top with alfalfa sprouts, watercress or lettuce leaves and drizzle additional dressing on top. Cover with top half of bun or roll.

TIPS: Refrigerate remaining dressing for later use.

For a lunch bag, pack tomato slices and dressing separately.

Nutrients per serving
Calories: 340
Protein: 17.4 g
Carbohydrate: 29.6 g
Fat: 17.7 g

Western Pitas

Makes 4 servings
Preparation: 10 minutes
Cooking: 5 minutes

2 tbsp	butter	30 mL
1/3 cup	finely chopped onion	75 mL
1/3 cup	finely chopped green pepper	75 mL
1/2 cup	chopped cooked ham	125 mL
6	eggs	6
	salt and cayenne pepper, to taste	
4	pita breads, cut in half	4
	mustard	
4	lettuce leaves	4
1 cup	shredded Monterey Jack or Cheddar cheese	250 mL

- In a medium nonstick skillet, melt butter over medium heat.
- Add onion and green pepper. Cook until soft, stirring frequently, about 5 minutes. Add ham.
- In a bowl, beat together eggs, salt and cayenne pepper with a fork. Pour into skillet.
- As mixture begins to set, gently move spatula across bottom and sides of skillet to form large, soft curds.
- Cook until eggs are thickened but still moist, and no visible liquid egg remains.
- Spread mustard inside pita halves. Spoon filling into pita halves and garnish with lettuce and cheese.

Nutrients per serving
Calories: 471
Protein: 26.3 g
Carbohydrate: 36.0 g
Fat: 24.0 g

Egg & Cheese Burgers

Makes 4 servings
Preparation: 10 minutes

5	hard-cooked eggs, peeled and finely chopped	5
1	green onion, finely chopped	1
6	stuffed olives, finely chopped	6
1/8 tsp	dry mustard	0.5 mL
	salt and cayenne pepper, to taste	
3 tbsp	mayonnaise	45 mL
4	hamburger buns	4
4	lettuce leaves	4
2	tomatoes, sliced	2
4	slices Brick or processed cheese	4

- In a bowl, combine eggs, green onion, olives, dry mustard, salt and cayenne pepper. Stir in mayonnaise.
- Place a lettuce leaf on each bun. Spread egg mixture evenly over lettuce. Top with tomato slices and cheese. Cover with top of bun.

Nutrients per serving
Calories: 492
Protein: 20.9 g
Carbohydrate: 36.8 g
Fat: 28.9 g

Bagel & Egg Melts

Makes 4 servings
Preparation: 10 minutes
Cooking: 5 minutes

6	hard-cooked eggs, peeled and coarsely chopped	6
1/2 cup	diced cooked ham	125 mL
1/3 cup	mayonnaise	75 mL
1 tbsp	chopped green onion	15 mL
	salt and pepper, to taste	
4	bagels or English muffins, cut in half	4
1/2 cup	shredded old Cheddar cheese	125 mL

Nutrients per serving
Calories: 584
Protein: 25.6 g
Carbohydrate: 51.2 g
Fat: 29.8 g

- In a bowl, combine eggs, ham, mayonnaise and green onion. Season with salt and pepper.
- Toast bagels or English muffins.
- Spread egg salad on top of each half and sprinkle with cheese.
- Grill in toaster oven or under broiler until cheese bubbles. Serve hot.

TIP: Instead of grilling sandwiches in toaster oven or under broiler, you can warm them in microwave on 'Medium' (50%) for 30 seconds.

Egg Pizza Roll-Ups

Makes 4 servings
Preparation: 15 minutes
Cooking: 10 minutes

8	eggs	8
3/4 cup	thick pizza sauce, divided	175 mL
	salt and pepper, to taste	
	pinch basil	
	pinch oregano	
1/2 tsp	butter	2 mL
4	7-inch (17 cm) pita breads	4
1 1/2 cups	shredded Mozzarella cheese	375 mL
1	green pepper, cut into 1/2-inch (1 cm) cubes	1
1 cup	sliced fresh mushrooms	250 mL
	cayenne pepper, to taste	

- In a small bowl, combine eggs, 1/4 cup (50 mL) pizza sauce, salt, pepper, basil and oregano. Beat with a fork until eggs are blended.

- Melt butter in a 6-inch (15 cm) skillet, over medium-high heat. Pour in 1/4 cup (50 mL) egg mixture.

- As eggs begin to set, lift edges to allow liquid egg to run under omelet. When set, slip spatula under omelet and slide it out of skillet.

- Repeat with remaining egg mixture.

- With a small sharp knife, cut around pita breads and separate halves. Lie flat on work surface.

- Place an omelet on each pita round. Spread 1 tbsp (15 mL) pizza sauce over each. Sprinkle with cheese. Arrange a few pepper pieces and mushroom slices in a row on each omelet. Sprinkle with cayenne pepper.

- Fold pita bread over and roll up tightly. Serve immediately or, to melt cheese, cover in plastic wrap and microwave on 'Medium' (50%) for 20 seconds. Serve hot or cold.

TIPS: Make omelets ahead, wrap individually and refrigerate for up to 2 days or freeze.

Ready-to-serve roll-ups can be covered in plastic wrap and kept refrigerated for one day. To reheat, place two roll-ups in microwave oven and cook on 'Medium' (50%) until hot, 30 to 45 seconds.

Variation: Roll-ups may also be sliced and served as appetizers.

Nutrients per serving
Calories: 519
Protein: 28.7 g
Carbohydrate: 45.0 g
Fat: 24.5 g

1

With a small sharp knife, cut around pita breads and separate halves.

2

Place an omelet on each pita round. Spread 1 tbsp (15 mL) pizza sauce over each. Top with cheese, peppers and mushrooms.

3

Fold pita bread over and roll up tightly.

Egg Croissant BLT

Makes 1 serving
Preparation: 5 minutes
Cooking: 5 minutes

2	slices lean bacon or bacon-style turkey, chopped	2
2	eggs	2
2 tbsp	milk	30 mL
	salt and pepper, to taste	
1	whole wheat croissant	1
2 tsp	mayonnaise	10 mL
	lettuce leaf	
1/2	tomato, sliced	1/2

- Fry bacon until almost crisp; drain and set aside.
- In a bowl, beat eggs with milk; season with salt and pepper.
- Pour into skillet with bacon and scramble over medium heat until set.
- Slice croissant in half. Spread mayonnaise over lower half. Place lettuce leaf on croissant. Spoon eggs onto lettuce and top with tomato slices. Cover with top half of croissant.

Nutrients per serving
Calories: 553
Protein: 26.2 g
Carbohydrate: 33.1 g
Fat: 34.7 g

Super Club Sandwiches

Makes 4 servings
Preparation: 15 minutes

1/4 cup	light mayonnaise	50 mL
1 tsp	Dijon mustard	5 mL
16	slices whole wheat bread, plain or toasted	16
4	thin slices turkey breast (or ham)	4
1	large tomato, thinly sliced	1
12	basil leaves (optional)	12
	lettuce leaves	
4	hard-cooked eggs, peeled and sliced	4
	salt and pepper, to taste	

Nutrients per serving
Calories: 453
Protein: 26.2 g
Carbohydrate: 56.1 g
Fat: 15.4 g

- In a small bowl, combine mayonnaise and mustard. Spread on one side of each slice of bread.
- Place turkey on top of 4 slices. Top with second layer of bread, tomato slices and basil leaves.
- Top with third layer of bread, lettuce leaves and hard-cooked egg slices. Season with salt and pepper. Cover with remaining slices of bread.
- Cut each sandwich into 4 wedges. Serve immediately.

TIP: To keep sandwiches for later, cover them with plastic wrap and refrigerate.

Variation: Substitute 4 kaiser or onion rolls, each split into 4 slices, for whole-wheat bread.

Quick Pizza Niçoise

Makes 4 servings
Preparation: 15 minutes
Cooking: 3 minutes

3	medium-size fresh tomatoes, seeded and cut into chunks	3
1/4 cup	fresh basil, shredded, or 1 tsp (5 mL) dried	50 mL
2	garlic cloves, minced	2
	salt and pepper, to taste	
1	14-oz (400 g) Italian style flatbread* or a 12-inch (30 cm) pizza crust, baked and cooled	1
4	hard-cooked eggs, peeled and cut into wedges	4
1/4 cup	sliced black olives	50 mL
1 cup	shredded Mozzarella cheese	250 mL
2 tbsp	grated Parmesan cheese	30 mL

*Or use 4 3.5-oz (100 g) Italian style flatbreads.

- In a bowl, combine tomatoes, basil, garlic, salt and pepper.
- Spoon evenly over bread. Place egg wedges over tomato mixture. Scatter black olives over pizza. Top with Mozzarella and Parmesan cheeses. Cut into 4 wedges.
- To warm, place on paper napkins or paper towels in microwave oven. Cook on 'High' (100%) until cheese is melted, 2 to 3 minutes.

Nutrients per serving
Calories: 474
Protein: 24.6 g
Carbohydrate: 54.2 g
Fat: 17.4 g

Oriental Egg Crepe on Bagel

Makes 4 servings
Preparation: 10 minutes
Cooking: 15 minutes

6	eggs	6
	salt and pepper, to taste	
1	medium onion, coarsely chopped	1
1	garlic clove, minced	1
1/2 cup	coarsely chopped red pepper	125 mL
1/2 cup	coarsely chopped green pepper	125 mL
3/4 cup	bean sprouts or shredded cabbage	175 mL
2 tsp	vegetable oil, divided	10 mL
2 tsp	soy sauce, divided	10 mL
4	bagels, cut in half (or onion buns, kaiser rolls or pita breads)	4
	chopped green onion, for garnish	

- In a bowl, beat together eggs, salt and pepper. Set aside. In another bowl, combine onion, garlic, red and green peppers, and bean sprouts; divide mixture in half to make 2 large crepes.

- Heat 1 tsp (5 mL) oil in a 10-inch (25 cm) nonstick skillet, over high heat. Add half the vegetables. Stir-fry 1 minute. Sprinkle with 1 tsp (5 mL) soy sauce and stir-fry 30 seconds longer. Reduce heat to medium. Pour half of the egg mixture (1/2 cup/ 125 mL) over vegetables in skillet.

- As eggs begin to set, tilt pan and lift edges of crepe to allow the uncooked egg to flow under. Remove crepe from heat and cut in half. Fold each half and place on bagel halves. Garnish with green onion. Cover with tops of bagels.

- Repeat with remaining ingredients to make 2 more sandwiches.

- Serve hot or at room temperature.

TIP: For a lunch bag, cool crepes completely. Assemble sandwiches, cover in plastic wrap and refrigerate. To reheat, remove plastic wrap, and place one sandwich on a paper napkin in microwave oven. Cook on 'High' (100%), 45 to 60 seconds.

Nutrients per sandwich
Calories: 367
Protein: 17.9 g
Carbohydrate: 47.8 g
Fat: 11.2 g

Western Clubhouse Sandwiches

A quick and delicious variation on an old favorite.

Makes 2 servings
Preparation: 10 minutes
Cooking: 10 minutes

2	slices ham, chopped	2
2 tbsp	chopped onion	30 mL
1/4 cup	chopped green pepper	50 mL
5	eggs	5
2 tbsp	water	30 mL
1/2 tsp	salt	2 mL
6	bread slices	6
	butter	
2	tomatoes, sliced	2
	lettuce leaves (enough for two sandwiches)	

Nutrients per serving
Calories: 602
Protein: 29.4 g
Carbohydrate: 52.6 g
Fat: 30.2 g

- In a skillet, sauté ham, onion and green pepper over moderate heat until vegetables are translucent.
- Meanwhile, in a small bowl, beat together eggs, water and salt.
- Pour egg mixture over cooked vegetables in skillet. Cook over low heat until eggs are almost set. Turn over and cook on other side. Cut into four wedges.
- Toast bread slices. Butter each slice.
- Top 1 slice of toast with 1 omelet wedge and half of the sliced tomatoes. Cover with another slice of toast.
- Cover the second slice of toast with half of the lettuce and a second omelet wedge. Top with third layer of toast.
- Cut sandwiches into four triangles and secure with toothpicks.
- Repeat for second sandwich.

Smoked Salmon Pizza

Makes 6 servings
Preparation: 5 minutes
Cooking: 10 minutes

3/4 cup	Cream cheese, softened	175 mL
1 tbsp	fresh dill or 1 tsp (5 mL) dried	15 mL
1	10 to 12-inch (25 to 30 cm) pre-baked, soft-type pizza crust	1
10	eggs	10
2 tbsp	milk	30 mL
	salt and pepper, to taste	
2 tbsp	butter	30 mL
6 oz	smoked salmon (or smoked turkey breast), thinly sliced	175 g
	fresh chives, chopped	

Nutrients per serving
Calories: 420
Protein: 21.4 g
Carbohydrate: 24.4 g
Fat: 25.8 g

- Blend Cream cheese and dill.
- Warm pizza crust according to package directions.
- In a bowl, beat eggs with milk. Season with salt and pepper.
- In a skillet, melt butter. Pour in egg mixture and cook over medium heat, stirring constantly. Cook until thickened, but still moist.
- Spread cheese over warm pizza crust. Top with eggs. Layer salmon (or turkey) slices over eggs and sprinkle with chives.
- Cut into wedges and serve immediately.

TIP: To prepare eggs in the microwave, cook on 'Medium-high' (70%) for 8 to 10 minutes, uncovered, stirring every 1 to 2 minutes.

Stuffed *Egg*stravaganza

Makes 8 servings
Preparation: 15 minutes
Cooking: 15 minutes

1	large French loaf, cut lengthwise and hollowed out	1
4 tbsp	butter, divided	60 mL
2 tbsp	mayonnaise	30 mL
8	slices ham	8
1	large tomato, sliced	1
1	small onion, thinly sliced	1
8	eggs, lightly beaten	8
	salt and pepper, to taste	
8	slices Cheddar cheese	8
2	dill pickles, sliced	2

- Preheat oven to 375°F (190°C).
- Spread the bread cavity with 2 tbsp (30 mL) each butter and mayonnaise.
- Line bread with ham slices. Top with tomato and onion.
- In a skillet, lightly scramble eggs in remaining butter. When still quite moist, pile eggs into bread. Season with salt and pepper. Top with cheese slices and dill pickles.
- Cover with top portion of bread. Wrap in greased foil and bake 15 to 20 minutes.
- Cut into thick slices to serve.

Variations: This recipe invites endless variations. You can substitute different varieties of breads, meats, cheeses and vegetables for the filling. (This is a great way to use leftovers.)

For individual servings, try using small amounts of filling in hollowed out dinner or kaiser rolls.

Nutrients per serving
Calories: 469
Protein: 23.6
Carbohydrate: 29.2
Fat: 28.3

1

Spread the bread cavity with 2 tbsp (30 mL) each butter and mayonnaise.

2

Line bread with ham slices. Top with tomato and onion.

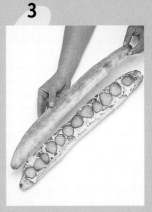

3

Pile the moist eggs into bread; season. Top with cheese slices and dill pickles. Cover with top portion of bread.

Egg Strudel

Makes 8 servings
Preparation: 10 minutes
Cooking: 35 minutes

1	10-oz (300 g) package frozen chopped spinach, thawed and squeezed dry	1
1 cup	finely chopped almonds (optional)	250 mL
1	onion, chopped	1
1	garlic clove, crushed	1
1/2 cup	melted butter, divided	125 mL
8	eggs	8
1 1/2 cups	grated Swiss cheese	375 mL
1 tsp	ground nutmeg	5 mL
1/2 tsp	ground allspice	2 mL
	salt and pepper, to taste	
1	16-oz (454 g) package strudel pastry (phyllo), thawed	1

- Preheat oven to 400°F (200°C).
- In a bowl, combine spinach and almonds.
- In a skillet, sauté onion and garlic in 1 tbsp (15 mL) butter. Add to spinach and almonds.
- In another bowl, beat eggs. Add cheese and seasonings.
- Line a greased 13 x 9-inch (33 cm x 23 cm) pan with 1 sheet of pastry, brush with some melted butter and repeat until there are 8 buttered sheets of pastry.
- Cover pastry with spinach mixture. Pour in egg and cheese mixture. Top with 4 more buttered sheets of pastry. Roll up edges and seal.
- Slit top of strudel. Brush with melted butter and bake 30 to 40 minutes or until pastry is golden and crisp.
- Cut strudel into thick slices and serve warm.

Nutrients per serving
Calories: 406
Protein: 17.3 g
Carbohydrate: 33.9 g
Fat: 22.1 g

1

Separate the crescent roll dough into four rectangles. Gently press diagonal perforations to seal.

2

Place 1/3 cup (75 mL) egg mixture on each dough rectangle.

3

Fold and pinch edges to seal.

Egg and Tuna Turnovers

Makes 4 servings
Preparation: 10 minutes
Cooking: 20 minutes

4	hard-cooked eggs, peeled and chopped	4
1/3 cup	flaked tuna	75 mL
1 tbsp	finely chopped onion	15 mL
1 tsp	parsley flakes (optional)	5 mL
	pinch dill seed (optional)	
1	10-oz (284 mL) can undiluted cream of celery soup	1
1	8-oz (225 g) package refrigerated crescent roll dough	1
1 tbsp	lemon juice	15 mL

- Preheat oven to 375°F (190°C).
- Thoroughly combine eggs, tuna, onion, parsley flakes, dill seed and one-third of the celery soup.
- Separate the crescent roll dough into four rectangles and place on a greased baking sheet. Gently press diagonal perforations to seal. Place 1/3 cup (75 mL) egg mixture on each rectangle. Fold and pinch edges to seal. Bake 20 minutes.
- Meanwhile, make a sauce by combining remaining soup and lemon juice in a saucepan. Heat to serving temperature and pour over baked turnovers.

Variations: Salmon, ham or chicken may be substituted for tuna. Cream of mushroom, cream of chicken or cream of asparagus soup may be used instead of cream of celery soup.

Nutrients per serving
Calories: 353
Protein: 14.5 g
Carbohydrate: 28.0 g
Fat: 20.4 g

Egg Pepperonata on Italian Flatbread

Makes 6 servings
Preparation: 10 minutes
Cooking: 20 minutes

1	large Italian flatbread*	1
1 tbsp	Dijon mustard	15 mL
6	eggs	6
	salt and pepper, to taste	
4 tsp	olive oil, divided	20 mL
1	medium onion, cut into wedges	1
1	large garlic clove, minced	1
1/2	red pepper, cut into strips	1/2
1/2	green pepper, cut into strips	1/2
1	medium tomato, cut into chunks	1
2 tbsp	chopped fresh basil or 1/2 tsp (2 mL) dried basil	30 mL
3/4 cup	shredded Mozzarella or Cheddar cheese	175 mL

* Or use focaccia, kaiser rolls or pita breads.

Nutrients per serving
Calories: 344
Protein: 16.7 g
Carbohydrate: 37.1 g
Fat: 14.1 g

- Preheat oven to 375°F (190°C).
- Split bread in half. Spread with mustard. Set aside.
- In a bowl, beat together eggs, salt and pepper. Heat 1 tsp (5 mL) olive oil in a large nonstick skillet, over medium-high heat. Add eggs.
- As egg mixture begins to set, gently move spatula across bottom and sides of skillet to form large, soft curds.
- When eggs are set but still moist, spoon over lower half of bread.
- Wipe skillet with a paper towel. Heat 1 tbsp (15 mL) olive oil over high heat. Add onion, garlic, red and green peppers, and tomato. Season with salt and pepper. Stir-fry until tender-crisp, about 2 minutes. Stir in basil.
- Spoon vegetable mixture over eggs. Sprinkle with cheese. Cover with top half of bread.
- Bake 10 minutes. Cut into individual portions. Serve hot or at room temperature.

TIP: For a lunch bag, cool pepperonata completely. Cover individual servings separately with plastic wrap and refrigerate. To reheat, remove plastic wrap and place one sandwich on a paper napkin in microwave. Reheat on 'High' (100%) 1 to 1 1/2 minutes.

Spicy Egg Fajitas

Makes 3 servings
Preparation: 10 minutes
Cooking: 10 minutes

4	eggs, lightly beaten	4
2 tbsp	drained and chopped pickled jalapeño peppers	30 mL
1/4 tsp	garlic salt	1 mL
1 tsp	vegetable oil	5 mL
1	small onion, cut into thin wedges	1
1/2	green pepper, cut into strips	1/2
6	flour tortillas	6
	salsa and guacamole, for garnish	

Nutrients per serving
Calories: 457
Protein: 17.2 g
Carbohydrate: 56.3 g
Fat: 18.2 g

- In a bowl, mix eggs, jalapeño peppers and garlic salt. Set aside.
- In a skillet, heat oil. Sauté onion and green pepper over medium heat until soft. Remove from pan and set aside.
- Pour half of egg mixture into pan and cook without stirring. When almost set, turn over briefly to finish cooking. Remove from pan, set aside and repeat with remaining egg mixture.
- Cut omelets into strips.
- To serve, place a few onion wedges, green pepper strips and egg strips in center of each tortilla. Top with about 1 tbsp (15 mL) each salsa and guacamole, then roll tortillas around the filling.

Variation: Replace jalepeño peppers with 1/2 tsp (2 mL) ground cumin.

QUICHES, CREPES AND OMELETS

With today's busy lifestyles, it's nice to know that eggs provide many quick and easy ways to serve complete and healthy meals.

Egg and Bacon Pie

Makes 6 servings
Preparation: 10 minutes
Cooking: 25 minutes

1	14-oz (400 g) package frozen puff pastry, thawed*	1
8 oz	back bacon or ham, thinly sliced	250 g
8	eggs	8
3 tbsp	finely chopped green onion, chives or onion	45 mL
1/2 tsp	salt	2 mL
1/4 tsp	pepper	1 mL
1 tbsp	water or milk	15 mL

*Or use pastry for a double-crust pie

- Preheat oven to 400°F (200°C).
- Divide puff pastry into two parts. Use one half to line a 9-inch (23 cm) quiche dish or pie plate.
- Arrange half of the back bacon or ham over the pastry base.
- Break 7 eggs into pie. Break yolks with fork but do not stir yolks and whites together.
- Sprinkle onion, salt and pepper over eggs. Top with remaining back bacon or ham and cover with remaining pastry.
- Beat remaining egg with water or milk and brush over top of pie.
- Bake 25 to 30 minutes.
- Serve hot or cold.

TIP: This pie is great for packed lunches.

Nutrients per serving
Calories: 435
Protein: 20.6 g
Carbohydrate: 25.1 g
Fat: 27.8 g

Florentine Multi-Layered Pie

Makes 8 servings
Preparation: 12 minutes
Cooking: 40 minutes

1 tbsp	butter or margarine	15 mL
1/4 cup	chopped onion	50 mL
1	garlic clove, minced	1
1	10-oz (300 g) package fresh spinach, rinsed and stems removed	1
3	eggs	3
1	egg, separated	1
	pastry for a 9-inch (23 cm) double-crust pie	
8 oz	thinly sliced cooked ham or turkey	250 g
1	red pepper, cut into strips	1
1	8-oz (227 g) package Swiss cheese or old Cheddar cheese, thinly sliced	1

Nutrients per serving
Calories: 407
Protein: 20.1 g
Carbohydrate: 21.7 g
Fat: 26.6 g

- Preheat oven to 400°F (200°C).

- In a large skillet, melt butter over medium heat. Add onion and garlic and sauté until soft. Add spinach, cover and cook just until spinach wilts. Drain well and set aside.

- In a bowl, whisk together 3 eggs and 1 egg white. Set aside.

- Line a 9-inch (23 cm) pie plate with pastry. Layer half the meat, red pepper, cheese and spinach mixture over pastry. Cover with half the beaten egg mixture. Repeat layers, pouring remaining egg mixture over top.

- Cover with pastry; seal and crimp the edges. Brush top with remaining egg yolk blended with a little water. Make a few small slits on the surface.

- Bake pie on cookie sheet 30 to 35 minutes, or until golden. Serve warm or cool.

All-Occasion Savory Quiche

Makes 8 servings
Preparation: 10 minutes
Cooking: 43 minutes

1	9-inch (23 cm) unbaked pie shell	1
4	eggs	4
1 1/2 cups	light cream (10%) or evaporated milk, undiluted	375 mL
1/2 tsp	salt	2 mL
1/4 tsp	pepper	1 mL
1/2–1 tsp	seasonings (see Variations)	2–5 mL
1 1/2–2 cups	filling ingredients (see Variations)	375–500 mL

- Preheat oven to 400°F (200°C).
- Partially bake pie shell on lowest rack in oven (8 minutes). Remove from oven and reduce heat to 350°F (180°C).
- In a bowl, lightly beat eggs, then add cream, salt, pepper and desired seasonings. Spread filling ingredients in partially baked shell. Pour in egg mixture.
- Bake 35 to 40 minutes. Let stand 5 to 10 minutes before serving.

Variations: Mushroom Quiche – 1 cup (250 mL) sliced mushrooms (sautéed), 1/2 cup (125 mL) shredded Cheddar cheese, 1/2 tsp (2 mL) dried basil.

Shrimp Quiche – 1 cup (250 mL) cooked shrimp or crabmeat, 3/4 cup (175 mL) shredded cheese, 1/4 cup (50 mL) chopped onion, 1/4 cup (50 mL) chopped green pepper, 1 tsp (5 mL) dried tarragon.

Corn Quiche – 1 cup (250 mL) fresh, canned (drained) or frozen (thawed) corn, 1/4 cup (50 mL) finely chopped onion and 1/2 tsp (2 mL) finely chopped parsley.

Nutrients per serving
Calories: 255
Protein: 10.8 g
Carbohydrate: 11.3 g
Fat: 18.5 g

1

Place ¾ cup (175 mL) cooked vegetables in the center of each omelet. Divide cheese among omelets.

2

Fold 4 sides of each omelet over filling to create a square envelope.

3

Slice in half diagonally and serve hot or at room temperature.

110

1

Place ¾ cup (175 mL) cooked vegetables in the center of each omelet. Divide cheese among omelets.

2

Fold 4 sides of each omelet over filling to create a square envelope.

3

Slice in half diagonally and serve hot or at room temperature.

110

Veggies in Golden Wrap

Makes 4 servings
Preparation: 10 minutes
Cooking: 10 minutes

3 cups	frozen mixed Oriental vegetables*	750 mL
1	green onion, chopped	1
3/4 tsp	Italian seasoning, divided	3 mL
	garlic powder, salt and pepper, to taste	
8	eggs	8
1/4 cup	water	50 mL
1 tsp	butter	5 mL
3/4 cup	shredded Cheddar or Mozzarella cheese	175 mL

* Or use 3 cups (750 mL) cooked fresh vegetables.

- Cook frozen vegetables in boiling salted water for 2 minutes. Drain. Add green onion, 1/4 tsp (1 mL) Italian seasoning, garlic powder, salt and pepper. Set aside.

- In a bowl, beat together eggs, water, 1/2 tsp (2 mL) Italian seasoning, salt and pepper.

- Melt butter in a 10-inch (25 cm) nonstick skillet over medium-high heat. Pour 1/2 cup (125 mL) egg mixture into skillet, tilting skillet to cover surface. Cook 2 to 2 1/2 minutes, or until set. Slide omelet from skillet. Repeat with remaining egg mixture to make 3 more omelets.

- Place 3/4 cup (175 mL) cooked vegetables in the center of each omelet. Divide cheese among omelets. Fold 4 sides of each omelet over filling to create a square envelope.

- Invert onto plates, slice in half diagonally and serve hot or at room temperature.

TIP: For a lunch bag, cool completely. Cover envelopes with plastic wrap and refrigerate. To reheat, remove plastic wrap, place one envelope on a plate and reheat in microwave oven on 'High' (100%) 30 to 60 seconds.

Nutrients per serving
Calories: 279
Protein: 20.0 g
Carbohydrate: 9.2 g
Fat: 18.2 g

Country Quiche

Makes 8 servings
Preparation: 15 minutes
Cooking: 25 minutes

2 tbsp	dried breadcrumbs	30 mL
2 cups	diced cooked ham, chicken or turkey	500 mL
1½ cups	chopped cooked vegetables	375 mL
½ cup	chopped green onion	125 mL
1½ cups	shredded Swiss or Cheddar cheese	375 mL
5	eggs	5
2 cups	milk	500 mL
½ tsp	salt	2 mL
	cayenne pepper, to taste	

- Preheat oven to 350°F (180°C).
- Sprinkle breadcrumbs over bottom of a well-buttered 15 x 10-inch (38 x 25 cm) jelly-roll pan.
- Scatter meat, vegetables, green onion and cheese in the pan.
- In a bowl, beat together eggs, milk, salt and cayenne pepper just until blended. Pour over ingredients in the pan.
- Bake in lower third of oven 25 minutes, or until egg mixture is just set. Do not overbake.
- Let stand 5 minutes. Cut into rectangles and serve hot, warm or at room temperature.

TIPS: For a lunch bag, cover quiche with plastic wrap; it may be reheated in microwave oven until just warm.

Cooked quiche may be refrigerated for up to three days or frozen for one month.

Variations: Sour cream, yogurt or even condensed cream soups (undiluted) may be substituted for part of the milk in the quiche.

Sprinkle chopped water chestnuts, parsley, pecans, walnuts or almonds over the uncooked quiche.

Nutrients per serving
Calories: 243
Protein: 20.9 g
Carbohydrate: 10.4 g
Fat: 12.9 g

Golden Cheddar Pancakes

Make 5 servings (3 pancakes per serving)
Preparation: 10 minutes
Cooking: 15 minutes

1³/₄ cups	whole wheat or all-purpose flour	425 mL
¹/₄ cup	sugar	50 mL
1 tbsp	baking powder	15 mL
¹/₂ tsp	salt	2 mL
¹/₈ tsp	ground cinnamon	0.5 mL
1¹/₂ cups	shredded old Cheddar or Colby cheese	375 mL
1	large apple, cored and diced	1
2	eggs	2
1¹/₄ cups	milk	300 mL
2 tbsp	melted butter	30 mL
1 tsp	vanilla extract	5 mL

- In a large bowl, combine flour, sugar, baking powder, salt and cinnamon. Stir in cheese and apple.

- In another bowl, beat together eggs, milk, butter and vanilla. Pour over dry ingredients and stir just until moistened.

- Lightly grease a nonstick skillet and heat over medium heat. Pour in ¹/₄ cup (50 mL) batter for each pancake, and spread into a 4-inch (10 cm) round. Cook until bubbles form on surface and underside is golden brown. Turn pancake and brown other side.

- Repeat to make additional pancakes. Serve warm, with syrup if desired.

Nutrients per serving
Calories: 450
Protein: 18.9 g
Carbohydrate: 51.7 g
Fat: 20.0 g

Broccoli and Dried Tomato Frittata

Makes 8 servings
Preparation: 15 minutes
Cooking: 20 minutes

8	sun-dried tomatoes (dry-packed)	8
10	eggs	10
1/2 cup	milk	125 mL
1/4 cup	minced fresh parsley	50 mL
1 tsp	dried basil	5 mL
1/2 tsp	salt	2 mL
1/4 tsp	pepper	1 mL
2 cups	chopped cooked broccoli	500 mL
2 tbsp	vegetable oil	30 mL
3/4 cup	shredded Cheddar or Swiss cheese	175 mL

- In a small bowl, soak dried tomatoes in very hot tap water until softened, 10 to 15 minutes. Drain and chop.
- In a large bowl, beat together eggs, milk, parsley, basil, salt and pepper until just blended. Stir in tomatoes and broccoli.

- In a 10-inch (25 cm) ovenproof skillet, heat oil over medium heat. Pour in egg mixture. Cook over low to medium heat until eggs are almost set but still moist on the surface, about 10 to 15 minutes. Occasionally lift edges to allow uncooked egg to flow to bottom of skillet.
- Sprinkle top with cheese. Place under broiler until cheese melts, 2 to 3 minutes. Frittata may be served hot, warm or cold. Cut into wedges to serve.

TIP: Instead of broiling, cheese can be melted by covering skillet with lid for a few minutes.

Nutrients per serving
Calories: 191
Protein: 12.4 g
Carbohydrate: 4.9 g
Fat: 13.7 g

Cheese and Vegetable Omelets

Makes 4 servings
Preparation: 5 minutes
Cooking: 5 minutes

8	eggs	8
2 tbsp	milk	30 mL
1/2 tsp	salt	2 mL
1/4 tsp	pepper	1 mL
4 tsp	butter	20 mL
2 cups	sautéed mushrooms or other cooked vegetables	500 mL
1/2 cup	shredded old Cheddar, Swiss or Monterey Jack cheese	125 mL

Nutrients per serving
Calories: 282
Protein: 18.0 g
Carbohydrate: 5.9 g
Fat: 21.0 g

- In a bowl, beat together eggs, milk, salt and pepper with a fork.

- In an 8-inch (20 cm) nonstick skillet, melt 1 tsp (5 mL) butter over medium-high heat. Pour in 1/2 cup (125 mL) egg mixture.

- As eggs begin to set at edges, use a spatula to gently push cooked portions to the center, tilting skillet to allow uncooked egg to flow into empty spaces.

- When almost set on surface but still moist, fill half of omelet with 1/2 cup (125 mL) vegetables and sprinkle with 2 tbsp (30 mL) cheese. Slip spatula under unfilled side, fold over filling and slide onto serving plate.

- Repeat to prepare 3 additional omelets.

California Omelet

Makes 6 servings
Preparation: 5 minutes
Cooking: 5 minutes

8	eggs	8
2 tbsp	milk	30 mL
2 tbsp	finely chopped fresh parsley	30 mL
3/4 tsp	Italian seasoning	3 mL
	salt and pepper, to taste	
2 tbsp	butter	30 mL
1/2 cup	salsa	125 mL
1	avocado, peeled and sliced (optional)	1
	lemon juice	
1 cup	shredded Swiss or Mozzarella cheese	250 mL

Nutrients per serving
Calories: 212
Protein: 14.1 g
Carbohydrate: 2.9 g
Fat: 15.8 g

- Preheat broiler.
- In a bowl, beat together eggs, milk and seasonings with a fork.
- In a 10-inch (25 cm) nonstick ovenproof skillet, melt butter over medium-high heat. Pour in egg mixture.
- As eggs begin to set at edges, use a spatula to gently push cooked portions to the center, tilting skillet to allow uncooked egg to flow into empty spaces.
- When eggs are almost set on surface but still look moist, spoon salsa on top and garnish with avocado slices sprinkled with lemon juice. Top with cheese.
- Place skillet under broiler, until cheese is just melted, about 30 seconds.
- Cut omelet into wedges and serve.

TIP: If handle of skillet is not ovenproof, wrap it with a double layer of heavy-duty aluminum foil.

All-in-One Potato Frittata

Makes 4 servings
Preparation: 10 minutes
Cooking: 20 minutes

1	medium potato, peeled and diced	1
8	eggs	8
1/2 cup	milk, chicken broth or water	125 mL
1/2 tsp	dried basil	2 mL
1/2 tsp	salt	2 mL
	pepper, to taste	
2 tbsp	vegetable oil	30 mL
1	medium onion, chopped	1
1/2	*each* green and red peppers, diced (or 1 small zucchini, diced)	1/2
1	garlic clove, minced	1
1/2 cup	shredded old Cheddar or Swiss cheese	125 mL

Nutrients per serving
Calories: 331
Protein: 18.3 g
Carbohydrate: 14.4 g
Fat: 22.2 g

- Preheat broiler.
- Cook potato in salted boiling water until tender, about 10 minutes. Drain.
- In a bowl, beat together eggs, milk, basil, salt and pepper until eggs are just blended.
- In a 10-inch (25 cm) ovenproof skillet, heat oil over medium heat. Add onion, peppers and garlic. Sauté 3 minutes. Add potato and sauté 2 minutes longer.
- Pour eggs over vegetables in skillet. Cook over low to medium heat until eggs are almost set but still moist on the surface, about 10 to 12 minutes. Occasionally lift edges to allow uncooked egg to run to bottom of skillet.
- Sprinkle top with cheese. Place under broiler until cheese melts, 2 to 3 minutes. Cut into wedges to serve.

TIP: If handle of skillet is not ovenproof, wrap it with a double layer of heavy-duty aluminum foil.

Frittata San Remo

Makes 4 servings
Preparation: 10 minutes
Cooking: 14 minutes

8	eggs	8
1/2 tsp	hot pepper sauce	2 mL
1/4 tsp	salt	1 mL
1	14-oz (398 mL) can artichoke hearts, drained and sliced	1
1/3 cup	roasted sweet pimentos, drained and chopped	75 mL
1 1/2 cups	finely shredded Mozzarella cheese	375 mL
2 tbsp	olive oil	30 mL
2	garlic cloves, minced	2
2 tbsp	shredded Cheddar cheese	30 mL

- Preheat broiler.
- In a large bowl, whisk eggs with hot pepper sauce and salt. Stir in artichoke slices, pimentos and Mozzarella cheese. In a 10-inch (25 cm) ovenproof skillet, heat oil over medium heat; add garlic and sauté for 2 minutes.
- Pour egg mixture into skillet and cook over medium-low heat until eggs are almost set but still moist on the surface, about 10 to 12 minutes. Occasionally lift edges to allow uncooked egg to run to bottom of skillet. Place under broiler 2 to 3 minutes or until set.
- To serve, loosen frittata edges with spatula. Place large warm plate over skillet and invert frittata onto plate. Place a warm serving plate on frittata and invert again so that top is up. Cut into wedges to serve. Garnish with shredded Cheddar cheese.

TIPS: If handle of skillet is not ovenproof, wrap it with a double layer of heavy-duty aluminum foil.

Spray cheese grater with cooking spray before shredding cheese. Cheese will slide easily.

Nutrients per serving
Calories: 396
Protein: 25.1 g
Carbohydrate: 10.3 g
Fat: 28.6 g

Puffy Omelet

Makes 1 serving
Preparation: 8 minutes
Cooking: 15 minutes

2	eggs	2
2 tsp	water	10 mL
	salt and pepper, to taste (optional)	
2 tbsp	sugar (optional)	30 mL

- Preheat oven to 350°F (180°C).
- Separate egg yolks and whites.
- Add water to yolks. Using an electric mixer, beat yolks until thick and lemon-colored. If omelet is to be served as a main course, season with salt and pepper.
- In a bowl, beat egg whites until soft peaks form. If omelet is to be served for dessert, gradually beat in sugar. Continue beating until whites are stiff but not dry. Fold yolk mixture carefully into egg whites.
- Pour omelet mixture into moderately hot, well-buttered 8-inch (20 cm) ovenproof skillet; level surface gently. Cook over low heat on top of stove until puffy and lightly browned on bottom, about 5 minutes. Lift omelet at edges to check color.
- Bake 8 to 10 minutes, or until a knife inserted in center comes out clean.
- To serve, score omelet just off center, fold and serve at once.

TIPS: For a fluffier puffy omelet, add a pinch of cornstarch to egg whites before beating them.

Water is preferred to milk when making omelets. The water turns to steam, producing a light, airy omelet.

If handle of skillet is not ovenproof, wrap it with a double layer of heavy-duty aluminum foil.

Variation: Try this omelet with a tasty filling or sauce (see page 21).

Nutrients per serving
Calories: 149
Protein: 12.5 g
Carbohydrate: 1.2 g
Fat: 10.0 g

Vegetable Strata

Makes 4 servings
Preparation: 10 minutes
Cooking: 30 minutes
Refrigeration: 4 hours

	cooking spray	
6	slices whole wheat bread, crusts removed	6
2 cups	frozen mixed vegetables (i.e., Italian, Oriental, etc.)	500 mL
6	eggs	6
1 cup	milk	250 mL
1/2 tsp	seasoned salt	2 mL
1/2 tsp	dry mustard	2 mL
1/2 tsp	dried basil	2 mL
1 cup	shredded Swiss cheese	250 mL
1 cup	frozen hash brown potatoes	250 mL

- Lightly spray a 9-inch (23 cm) square pan with cooking spray. Arrange bread slices, slightly overlapping, on bottom of pan.
- Place vegetables over bread; set aside.
- In a large bowl, beat together eggs, milk, seasoned salt, dry mustard and basil. Pour over vegetables. Sprinkle with cheese and hash brown potatoes.
- Cover and refrigerate at least 4 hours or overnight.
- Preheat oven to 375°F (190°C).
- Bake 30 minutes. Serve warm.

TIP: If you do not have frozen hash brown potatoes, use 1 cup (250 mL) soft whole wheat bread cubes instead.

Nutrients per serving
Calories: 424
Protein: 26.1 g
Carbohydrate: 42.0 g
Fat: 17.8 g

Greek Omelet

This puffy omelet is a cross between an Italian frittata and a French omelet. The mixture of earthy Greek flavors is a favorite.

Makes 3 servings
Preparation: 5 minutes
Cooking: 5 minutes

4	eggs	4
2 tbsp	water	30 mL
	hot pepper sauce, to taste	
	freshly ground pepper, to taste	
1 tbsp	olive oil	15 mL
4	green onions, trimmed and chopped	4
1	plum tomato, seeded and chopped	1
1 tbsp	chopped fresh mint	15 mL
2 oz	Feta cheese, crumbled	60 g

- In a bowl, beat together eggs, water, hot pepper sauce and pepper.
- In a large nonstick skillet, heat oil over high heat.
- Pour in egg mixture and cook over medium-high heat until edges are just set.
- Sprinkle green onions, tomato, mint and Feta over eggs.
- Reduce heat to low and cook until eggs are nearly set.
- Using two spatulas, flip over opposite sides of omelet to meet in center. Turn out onto platter and serve.

Nutrients per serving
Calories: 201
Protein: 11.6 g
Carbohydrate: 4.0 g
Fat: 15.4 g

Cheesy Spinach Crepes

Makes 4 servings
Preparation: 20 minutes
Cooking: 28 minutes
Standing: 30 minutes

Crepes

3	eggs	3
1 cup	milk	250 mL
1 tbsp	melted butter	15 mL
3/4 cup	all-purpose flour	175 mL
1/4 tsp	salt	1 mL

Cheese Filling

2 cups	shredded Havarti, Swiss or Mozzarella cheese, divided	500 mL
2 cups	Cottage or Ricotta cheese	500 mL
1/4 cup	grated Parmesan cheese	50 mL
1	egg, lightly beaten	1
1	10-oz (300 g) package frozen chopped spinach, thawed and squeezed dry	1
1/4 tsp	salt	1 mL
1/8 tsp	pepper	0.5 mL

Topping

1 1/2 cups	tomato sauce	375 mL

Crepes

- Blend crepe ingredients in a blender or food processor for 5 seconds. Scrape down sides and blend 20 seconds longer. Cover and let stand at least 30 minutes.

- Heat an 8-inch (20 cm) nonstick skillet over medium heat; grease lightly. Stir batter. Pour 3 tbsp (45 mL) batter into pan and quickly tip pan to coat bottom. Cook until bottom is slightly browned, about 45 seconds. Turn crepe with spatula and cook about 20 seconds longer. Transfer to a plate.

- Repeat with remaining batter, greasing skillet lightly before cooking each crepe. Makes 10 to 12 crepes. Select 10 crepes.

Filling

- Reserve 1/2 cup (125 mL) Havarti cheese. Combine remaining filling ingredients. Place 1/3 cup (75 mL) cheese filling on each crepe and roll up.

- Preheat oven to 375°F (190°C).

- Place rolled crepes seam-side down in a greased 13 x 9-inch (33 x 23 cm) baking dish. Pour tomato sauce over top. Sprinkle with reserved Havarti cheese. Bake 20 to 25 minutes.

TIP: Crepe recipe can be doubled if desired and prepared ahead. Separate crepes with pieces of waxed paper and cover in plastic wrap. Keep refrigerated for up to 3 days or wrap in foil and freeze. Crepes may be stuffed and rolled a day ahead. Top with sauce just before baking.

Nutrients per serving
Calories: 610
Protein: 49.3 g
Carbohydrate: 37.4 g
Fat: 29.3 g

Easy Layered Omelet Cake

Makes 6 servings
Preparation: 35 minutes
Cooking: 45 minutes
Standing: 15 minutes

Omelets

10	eggs	10
1/4 cup	water	50 mL
	salt, pepper and hot pepper sauce, to taste	
1 tsp	butter, melted	5 mL

Cheese Sauce

3 tbsp	butter	45 mL
3 tbsp	flour	45 mL
11/2 cups	milk	375 mL
	salt, pepper and ground nutmeg, to taste	
11/2 cups	shredded old Cheddar cheese	375 mL

Filling

1 tbsp	butter	15 mL
1	small onion, finely chopped	1
2	10-oz (300 g) packages frozen spinach, thawed and squeezed dry	2

Nutrients per serving
Calories: 379
Protein: 22.1 g
Carbohydrate: 1.8 g
Fat: 27.3 g

- Preheat oven to 375°F (190°C).

Omelets

- In a bowl, beat together eggs, water and seasonings. In a 9-inch (23 cm) nonstick skillet, melt butter over medium-high heat. Pour 2/3 cup (150 mL) egg mixture into skillet, tilting skillet to cover surface. Cook 2 to 21/2 minutes or until set. Slide omelet from skillet. Repeat to make 3 more omelets.

Cheese Sauce

- In a medium saucepan over medium heat, melt butter. Stir in flour and cook 1 minute. Stir in milk; cook, stirring, until mixture is thickened. Reduce heat and simmer 2 minutes, stirring occasionally. Season with salt, pepper and nutmeg. Stir in 1 cup (250 mL) cheese until smooth. Remove from heat.

Filling

- In a large skillet, melt butter over medium heat. Add onion; cook 3 minutes. Add spinach and cook over medium-high heat until liquid is evaporated. Stir in 1 cup (250 mL) cheese sauce. Adjust seasoning.

- Place one omelet in a greased 9-inch (23 cm) spring-form pan. Alternate 3 layers of spinach filling and omelets, ending with an omelet on top. Top with remaining sauce and cheese.

- Place pan on a baking sheet and bake until top is golden and mixture is hot, 35 to 45 minutes. Cover and let stand 15 minutes. Remove sides of pan. Serve in wedges.

TIP: Omelets, cheese sauce and filling can be prepared two days in advance. Keep separately in the refrigerator and assemble completely the night before baking.

1

Place one omelet in a greased 9-inch (23 cm) spring-form pan.

2

Alternate 3 layers of spinach filling and omelets, ending with an omelet on top.

3

Top with remaining sauce and cheese.

Zucchini Frittata

Served with a salad and some crusty bread, frittatas make a great weeknight family dinner.

Makes 6 servings
Preparation: 5 minutes
Cooking: 8 minutes

8	eggs	8
2	medium zucchini, trimmed and grated	2
4 oz	thinly sliced prosciutto (or ham), torn into shreds	125 g
1/4 cup	grated Parmesan cheese	50 mL
3 tbsp	chopped fresh Italian parsley	45 mL
	salt and freshly ground pepper, to taste	
1 tbsp	olive oil	15 mL

Nutrients per serving
Calories: 178
Protein: 3.6 g
Carbohydrate: 13.9 g
Fat: 11.8 g

- Preheat broiler.
- In a large mixing bowl, beat eggs. Add zucchini, prosciutto, Parmesan, parsley, salt and pepper. Mix to combine.
- In a large nonstick or cast-iron ovenproof skillet, heat oil over medium-high heat. Pour in egg mixture and swirl to set evenly. Smooth top with a fork.
- Reduce heat to medium-low and cook, uncovered, until edges are set and center is runny.
- Place under broiler briefly, just to set (1 to 2 minutes). Set aside to cool in pan 5 minutes.
- Slide onto a platter to serve. Cut into wedges and serve warm or at room temperature.

TIP: If handle of skillet is not ovenproof, wrap it with a double layer of heavy-duty aluminum foil.

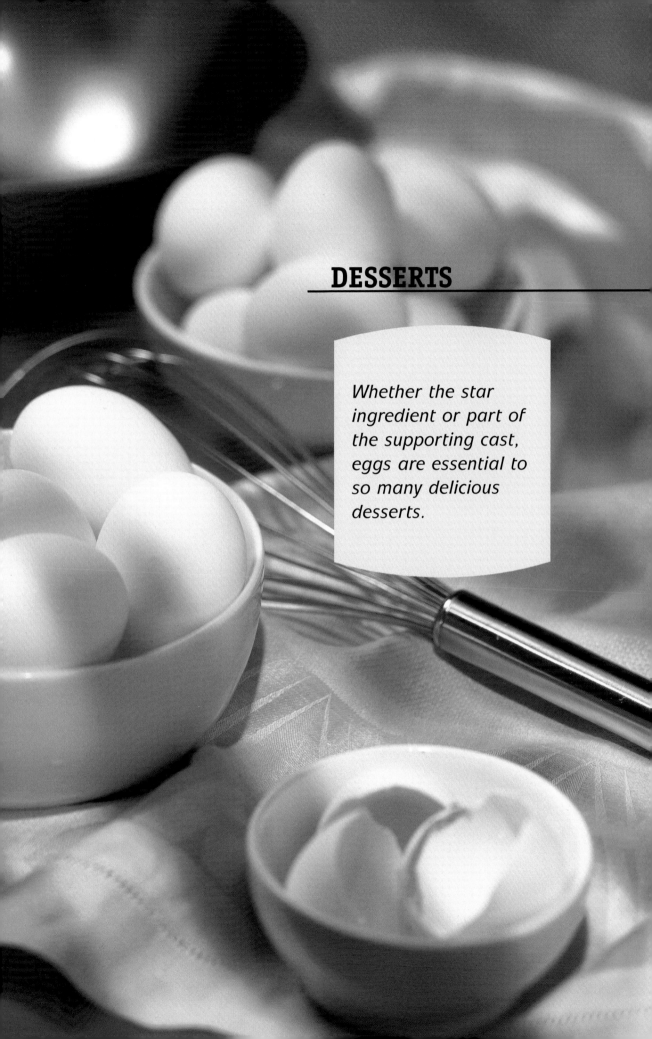

DESSERTS

Whether the star ingredient or part of the supporting cast, eggs are essential to so many delicious desserts.

Cocoa Brownies

These moist, fudgy brownies are lower in fat than most brownies because they are made with cocoa instead of chocolate.

Makes 16 squares
Preparation: 8 minutes
Cooking: 20 minutes

1/2 cup	soft margarine	125 mL
1 cup	sugar	250 mL
1/2 cup	all-purpose flour	125 mL
1/2 cup	cocoa	125 mL
1 tsp	baking powder	5 mL
1 tsp	vanilla extract	5 mL
4	egg whites	4

- Preheat oven to 325°F (160°C).
- In a bowl, use an electric mixer to beat margarine and sugar until light and creamy. Beat in flour, cocoa, baking powder and vanilla.
- In another bowl, beat egg whites until they are snowy white and hold their shape. With a rubber spatula, fold beaten whites into cocoa mixture until completely blended.
- Pour into a greased and floured 8-inch (20 cm) square baking pan. Bake 20 to 25 minutes. Brownies should be slightly underbaked in the middle and firm to the touch near the edges.
- Cool completely before cutting.

Nutrients per square
Calories: 126
Protein: 1.8 g
Carbohydrate: 17.0 g
Fat: 6.4 g

Carrot Cake

This moist, low-fat carrot cake is delicious as is or with a light lemon frosting.

Makes 18 servings
Preparation: 8 minutes
Cooking: 40 minutes

3	eggs	3
1 cup	packed brown sugar	250 mL
1/4 cup	vegetable oil	50 mL
3/4 cup	plain low-fat yogurt	175 mL
1 cup	all-purpose flour	250 mL
1 cup	whole wheat flour	250 mL
2 tsp	baking powder	10 mL
1/2 tsp	baking soda	2 mL
1/2 tsp	salt	2 mL
2 tsp	ground cinnamon	10 mL
1 tsp	ground ginger	5 mL
1/2 tsp	ground nutmeg	2 mL
3 cups	grated raw carrots	750 mL
1 cup	drained crushed pineapple	250 mL
1 cup	raisins	250 mL

- Preheat oven to 350°F (180°C).

- In a large bowl, beat eggs until frothy; beat in brown sugar, then oil and yogurt. Add both flours, baking powder, baking soda, salt, cinnamon, ginger and nutmeg; mix thoroughly. Stir in carrots, pineapple and raisins. Pour into a greased and floured tube pan or a 13 x 9-inch (33 x 23 cm) rectangular pan.

- Bake 75 minutes if using a tube pan or 40 to 50 minutes if using a rectangular pan, or until tester inserted in center comes out clean.

Nutrients per serving
Calories: 183
Protein: 3.8 g
Carbohydrate: 34.0 g
Fat: 4.3 g

Chocolate and Caramel Flan

Makes 8 servings
Preparation: 10 minutes
Cooking: 55 minutes

Caramel

1/2 cup	sugar	125 mL
1/4 cup	cold water	50 mL
1/3 cup	cold water	75 mL

Flan

1/2 cup	sugar	125 mL
4	eggs	4
2	egg yolks	2
1 tsp	Tia Maria (optional)	5 mL
2 oz	bittersweet chocolate, melted	60 g
2 cups	hot milk	500 mL

Nutrients per serving
Calories: 215
Protein: 6.6 g
Carbohydrate: 30.2 g
Fat: 8.7 g

- Preheat oven to 350°F (180°C).

- To make caramel, heat sugar and 1/4 cup (50 mL) cold water in a saucepan over medium-high heat. Stir only until the mixture starts to boil.

- Once the sugar becomes caramel-colored, quickly add 1/3 cup (75 mL) cold water. Continue cooking 30 seconds.

- Pour three-quarters of the caramel into a round 8-inch (20 cm) baking dish. With a wooden spoon, spread it out evenly using a circular motion. Reserve the rest of the caramel.

- In a stainless steel bowl, beat sugar, eggs, egg yolks and Tia Maria, if using. Do not allow the mixture to become foamy.

- In another bowl, beat the melted chocolate with the hot milk. Incorporate into the egg mixture, beating continuously. Pour the mixture through a strainer into the baking dish, over the caramel. Place in a baking dish filled half-full with hot water. Bake 45 minutes.

- Remove from oven and cool before refrigerating. Serve slices of flan with reserved caramel.

Strawberry Pavlova

Makes 8 servings
Preparation: 10 minutes
Cooking: 1 hour, 20 minutes

4	eggs, separated	4
1 tsp	vanilla extract	5 mL
1/4 tsp	cream of tartar	1 mL
1/4 tsp	salt	1 mL
11/3 cups	sugar, divided	325 mL
1/3 cup	lemon juice	75 mL
1 cup	whipping cream	250 mL
4 cups	sliced strawberries	1 L

- Preheat oven to 250°F (120°C).
- Line a cookie sheet with foil. Draw a 9-inch (23 cm) circle on it.
- In a large glass or metal bowl, beat egg whites, vanilla, cream of tartar and salt at highest speed of electric mixer until soft peaks form. Gradually beat in 1 cup (250 mL) sugar, 2 tbsp (30 mL) at a time, beating well after each addition; continue beating until stiff, glossy peaks form.

- Spoon onto prepared cookie sheet within the circle, with edges piled higher than center. Bake for 11/4 to 11/2 hours until crisp on the outside and firm to the touch. Turn off heat and allow to cool in oven with oven door propped open.
- Meanwhile, in a heavy saucepan, whisk together egg yolks, remaining 1/3 cup (75 mL) sugar and lemon juice. Cook over low heat, stirring constantly, 5 to 6 minutes or until thickened and smooth. Cover surface directly with plastic wrap; cool.
- Whip cream until stiff; fold in cooled lemon mixture. Just before serving, spread whipped cream mixture over meringue. Top with strawberries and serve.

Nutrients per serving
Calories: 289
Protein: 4.2 g
Carbohydrate: 40.3 g
Fat: 13.2 g

Lemon Meringue Pie

Makes 6 servings
Preparation: 5 minutes
Cooking: 20 minutes

Filling

1¼ cups	sugar	300 mL
1/3 cup	cornstarch	75 mL
1½ cups	boiling water	375 mL
2 tsp	grated lemon rind	10 mL
1/3 cup	lemon juice	75 mL
3	egg yolks	3
2 tbsp	butter	30 mL

Meringue

3	egg whites	3
1/4 tsp	lemon juice	1 mL
1/4 cup	sugar	50 mL
1/4 cup	flaked coconut	50 mL
1	9-inch (23 cm) baked pie shell	1

- Preheat oven to 325°F (160°C).

Filling

- In a medium saucepan, stir together sugar and cornstarch. Add boiling water, stirring well. Cook over direct heat, stirring constantly, until thick and clear. Stir in rind and lemon juice. Continue cooking and stirring until mixture comes to a boil. Remove from heat.
- In a small bowl, beat egg yolks. Gradually add half of hot lemon mixture, stirring constantly. Pour egg mixture into saucepan. Cook, stirring, for 1 minute. Remove from heat. Stir in butter until melted. Cool.

Meringue

- In a small bowl, beat egg whites with lemon juice until soft peaks form. Gradually beat in sugar, a spoonful at a time. Continue beating until meringue is stiff and glossy.
- Pour cooled filling into baked pie shell. Pile meringue over filling, being sure it meets the crust all around to prevent shrinking or weeping. Swirl meringue with back of spoon to form peaks. Sprinkle coconut on meringue. Bake 10 to 15 minutes, or until meringue is delicately browned.
- Cool at least an hour before serving. Store in refrigerator.

Microwave Directions

- In a 4-cup (1 L) microwaveable bowl, combine sugar and cornstarch. Gradually stir in water. Cook in microwave on 'High' (100%) 4 minutes or until mixture comes to a boil and thickens, stirring after 2 minutes.
- In a bowl, beat egg yolks. Whisk about a third of hot mixture into egg yolks; add egg yolk mixture to remaining hot mixture and blend well. Cook in microwave on 'High' (100%) 1 minute or until thickened. Stir in butter, lemon rind and juice. Pour into baked pie shell.
- Beat egg whites with lemon juice until frothy. Gradually beat in sugar until mixture forms stiff peaks. Spread over hot filling. Cook in microwave on 'Medium-High' (70%) 3 to 4 minutes, or until set.
- Spread coconut in a shallow microwaveable dish. Cook in microwave on 'Medium-High' (70%) 3 to 4 minutes or until lightly browned, stirring several times. Cool. Sprinkle coconut on meringue.

Nutrients per serving
Calories: 419
Protein: 4.3 g
Carbohydrate: 69.7 g
Fat: 14.4 g

Mocha Chiffon Cake

Makes 12 servings
Preparation: 15 minutes
Cooking: 1 hour
Refrigeration: 1 hour

Cake

2 tsp	instant coffee powder or granules	10 mL
3/4 cup	hot water	175 mL
1 3/4 cups	all-purpose flour	425 mL
1 1/2 cups	sugar	375 mL
1 tbsp	baking powder	15 mL
1/2 tsp	salt	2 mL
1/2 cup	vegetable oil	125 mL
6	egg yolks	6
1 tsp	vanilla extract	5 mL
6	egg whites	6
1/2 tsp	cream of tartar	2 mL
2	1-oz (28 g) squares semi-sweet chocolate, grated	2

Cocoa Whipped Cream

2 cups	whipping cream	500 mL
1/3 cup	sugar	75 mL
3 tbsp	cocoa	45 mL
1 tsp	vanilla extract	5 mL

chocolate eggs or semi-sweet chocolate curls, for garnish

- Preheat oven to 325°F (160°C).

Cake

- Dissolve coffee powder or granules in hot water; cool to room temperature.
- In a large bowl, combine flour, sugar, baking powder and salt; stir until well mixed. Make a well in center; add oil, egg yolks, vanilla and cooled coffee. Beat with a wooden spoon until smooth.
- In another large bowl, use electric mixer to beat egg whites and cream of tartar until stiff but not dry.
- Pour batter over egg whites; fold in carefully, adding grated chocolate towards the end. Spoon batter into an ungreased 10-inch (25 cm) tube pan.
- Bake 60 to 70 minutes, or until cake springs back when lightly touched. Turn pan upside down and let cake hang until cool. Remove from pan.

Cocoa Whipped Cream

- In a medium bowl, combine whipping cream, sugar, cocoa powder and vanilla. Stir to blend ingredients, but do not beat. Cover and refrigerate 1 to 2 hours. Whip until soft peaks form.
- Frost cake with cocoa whipped cream. Decorate with chocolate eggs or semi-sweet chocolate curls. Refrigerate until ready to serve.

Nutrients per serving
Calories: 466
Protein: 6.4 g
Carbohydrate: 49.8 g
Fat: 27.8 g

Toasted Almond Soufflé

Makes 4 servings
Preparation: 25 minutes
Cooking: 48 minutes

Soufflé

2 tbsp	butter	30 mL
3 tbsp	all-purpose flour	45 mL
	pinch salt	
1/2 cup	table cream	125 mL
3/4 tsp	grated orange rind	3 mL
1/4 cup	orange juice	50 mL
3	eggs, separated	3
1/4 cup	finely chopped toasted almonds	50 mL
3 tbsp	sugar	45 mL

Strawberry-Orange Sauce

3 tbsp	sugar	45 mL
1 1/2 tsp	cornstarch	7 mL
	pinch salt	
1/2 cup	orange juice	125 mL
2 tbsp	butter	30 mL
1 cup	fresh strawberries, cut into quarters	250 mL

Nutrients per serving
Calories: 366
Protein: 8.3 g
Carbohydrate: 31.4 g
Fat: 23.9 g

- Preheat oven to 325°F (160°C).

Soufflé

- In a small saucepan, melt butter over medium-low heat. Stir in flour and salt and cook 1 minute. Add cream and cook 1 more minute, until bubbly. Remove from heat. Stir in orange rind and juice.

- In a bowl, beat egg yolks on highest speed of electric mixer for 5 minutes. Gradually add orange mixture and mix well. Stir in almonds. Set aside.

- In a medium bowl, beat egg whites until soft peaks form; continue beating, adding sugar gradually, until stiff peaks form. Fold orange-almond mixture into egg whites.

- Pour into an ungreased 6-cup (1.5 L) soufflé dish. Bake 40 minutes.

Strawberry-Orange Sauce

- In a small saucepan, combine sugar, cornstarch and salt. Stir in orange juice and cook over medium heat until mixture thickens and bubbles.

- Remove from heat; stir in butter until melted. Stir in strawberries. Cover surface of sauce with plastic wrap. Let sauce stand at room temperature until ready to serve. Spoon 1/4 cup (50 mL) sauce over each serving of soufflé.

Maple Walnut Tarts

Makes 12 tarts
Preparation: 15 minutes
Cooking: 20 minutes

Flaky Pastry

2 cups	all-purpose flour	500 mL
2 tbsp	sugar	30 mL
1/2 tsp	salt	2 mL
1/4 tsp	baking powder	1 mL
1/2 cup	cold butter or hard margarine, cut into pieces	125 mL
1/3 cup	vegetable shortening, at room temperature	75 mL
1/2 cup	ice-cold water (approx.)	125 mL

Walnut Filling

3	eggs	3
1 cup	maple syrup	250 mL
3/4 cup	brown sugar, packed	175 mL
2 tbsp	butter or margarine, melted	30 mL
1 tsp	vanilla extract	5 mL
1 cup	coarsely chopped walnuts	250 mL

Nutrients per tart
Calories: 371
Protein: 4.7 g
Carbohydrate: 45.6 g
Fat: 19.7 g

- Preheat oven to 425°F (220°C).

Pastry

- In a medium bowl, combine flour, sugar, salt and baking powder. Cut in butter or margarine and shortening until mixture is crumbly. Add water, 2 tbsp (30 mL) at a time, mixing with a fork. Add a little more water if necessary. Press mixture into 2 flat disks. Wrap in waxed paper and refrigerate 30 minutes.

Filling

- In a bowl, beat together eggs, syrup, brown sugar, melted butter or margarine and vanilla until just blended.

- On a lightly floured board, roll pastry disks to 1/16 inch (1.5 mm). Cut into 5-inch (12 cm) circles. Line 12 3 1/2-inch (9 cm) tart pans with pastry.

- Divide walnuts and maple syrup mixture equally among tart shells. Bake 20 to 25 minutes, or until pastry is golden and filling is soft set.

- Let stand 15 minutes before removing from tart pans. Serve warm or at room temperature.

Luscious Lemon Cheese Pie

Makes 8 servings
Preparation: 10 minutes
Cooking: 50 minutes

Cheese Layer

1	8-oz (250 g) package regular or light Cream cheese, softened	1
1/2 cup	sugar	50 mL
1	egg	1
1	9-inch (23 cm) unbaked pie shell (if using frozen, use deep-dish style)	1

Lemon Layer

1/2 cup	corn syrup	125 mL
2 tsp	grated lemon rind	10 mL
1/3 cup	lemon juice	75 mL
2	eggs	2
2 tbsp	butter or margarine, melted	30 mL
1 tbsp	cornstarch	15 mL
	lemon rind, for garnish (optional)	

- Preheat oven to 350°F (180°C).

Cheese Layer

- In a bowl, beat Cream cheese and sugar until smooth. Add egg and blend well. Spread evenly in pie shell.

Lemon Layer

- In another bowl, beat corn syrup, lemon rind, lemon juice, eggs, butter or margarine and cornstarch until smooth. Pour over cheese layer.
- Bake 50 to 55 minutes, or until set and golden. Cool on rack. Garnish with lemon rind, if desired.

TIP: To prevent spillage, place pie on oven rack before adding lemon layer. Pour lemon filling into pie and bake as directed.

Nutrients per serving
Calories: 334
Protein: 5.5 g
Carbohydrate: 32.4 g
Fat: 20.8 g

Apple and Spice Bread Pudding

Makes 8 servings
Preparation: 15 minutes
Cooking: 45 minutes
Refrigeration: 4 hours

2 tbsp	butter or margarine	30 mL
2	medium apples, cored and chopped	2
	cooking spray	
3 cups	day-old white or whole wheat bread cubes	750 mL
1/2 cup	raisins	125 mL
4	eggs	4
2 cups	milk	500 mL
1/3 cup	packed brown sugar	75 mL
1 tsp	vanilla extract	5 mL
1/2 tsp	ground cinnamon	2 mL
1/4 tsp	ground nutmeg	1 mL

Nutrients per serving
Calories: 216
Protein: 6.6 g
Carbohydrate: 31.5 g
Fat: 7.7 g

- In a small saucepan, melt butter over medium heat. Stir in apples. Cover and cook over medium heat, stirring occasionally, until slightly softened, about 5 minutes.

- Spray a shallow 1½-quart (1.5 L) baking dish with cooking spray. Combine apples, bread cubes and raisins in dish.

- In a medium bowl, beat together eggs, milk, brown sugar, vanilla, cinnamon and nutmeg until sugar is dissolved. Pour over apple mixture. Cover and refrigerate at least 4 hours.

- Preheat oven to 350°F (180°C).

- Bake pudding until knife inserted in center comes out clean, about 45 to 55 minutes. Serve hot, warm or chilled.

Variation: For a delicious treat, serve pudding with warm cinnamon sauce. In a glass bowl or measuring cup, stir together 1 cup (250 mL) corn syrup and 1/2 tsp (2 mL) ground cinnamon. Microwave on 'High' (100%) 1 minute; stir. Pour over pudding.

Pineapple Cinnamon Coffee Cake

Makes 12 servings
Preparation: 10 minutes
Cooking: 50 minutes

Cinnamon Topping

3/4 cup	brown sugar	175 mL
3/4 cup	chopped walnuts	175 mL
1/3 cup	all-purpose flour	75 mL
1 1/2 tsp	ground cinnamon	7 mL
1/4 cup	butter or margarine	50 mL

Cake

1	19-oz (540 mL) can crushed pineapple	1
2 1/4 cups	all-purpose flour	550 mL
1 tbsp	grated lemon rind	15 mL
1 1/2 tsp	baking powder	7 mL
3/4 tsp	baking soda	3 mL
1/2 tsp	salt	2 mL
1/2 cup	butter or margarine	125 mL
1 cup	sugar	250 mL
3	eggs	3
1 cup	sour cream	250 mL

Nutrients per serving
Calories: 434
Protein: 6.3 g
Carbohydrate: 58.3 g
Fat: 20.6 g

- Preheat oven to 350°F (180°C).

Topping

- Combine brown sugar, walnuts, flour and cinnamon in a small bowl. Cut in butter or margarine until crumbly. Set aside.

Cake

- Place pineapple in a sieve, pressing fruit with a spoon to drain excess juice; set pineapple aside.

- In a medium bowl, combine flour, lemon rind, baking powder, baking soda and salt.

- In a large bowl, cream butter or margarine with sugar until well mixed. Add eggs, one at a time, beating well after each addition. Stir in dry ingredients alternately with sour cream.

- Spread half the batter in a greased and floured 10-inch (25 cm) square baking pan or 13 x 9-inch (33 x 23 cm) baking pan. Sprinkle half the cinnamon topping over batter. Spread remaining batter on top. Spoon pineapple evenly over batter. Sprinkle with remaining cinnamon topping.

- Bake until toothpick inserted in center comes out clean, about 50 minutes. Serve warm.

Variations: Substitute blueberry, cherry, raspberry or apple pie filling for crushed pineapple. You can also substitute 4 medium apples, peeled, cored and thinly sliced; arrange slices over batter, overlapping slightly. Sprinkle with remaining cinnamon topping and bake as directed.

Zabaglione

This light, easy Italian dessert is perfect for a
summer evening. Serve plain or topped with
sweetened berries or softly whipped cream.

Makes 4 servings
Preparation: 2 minutes
Cooking: 15 minutes

3	egg yolks	3
1/2 cup	sugar	125 mL
1/2 cup	sweet Marsala wine	125 mL

- In a double boiler or in a stainless steel bowl placed over simmering water, whisk together yolks and sugar until pale.
- Add Marsala, one spoonful at a time, whisking thoroughly between additions.
- Continue cooking over low heat, whisking constantly, until thick and creamy, about 10 minutes.
- Serve warm or chilled, in wine or cocktail glasses.

Nutrients per serving
Calories: 173
Protein: 2.2 g
Carbohydrate: 28.6 g
Fat: 4.0 g

Cranberry Pecan Pie

Makes 8 servings
Preparation: 5 minutes
Cooking: 50 minutes

3	eggs, lightly beaten	3
1 cup	corn syrup	250 mL
2/3 cup	sugar	150 mL
2 tbsp	butter or margarine, melted	30 mL
1 tsp	vanilla extract	5 mL
1 cup	pecan halves	250 mL
1 cup	fresh or frozen cranberries, cut in half	250 mL
1 tbsp	grated orange rind	15 mL
1	9-inch (23 cm) unbaked pastry shell	1
	whipped cream (optional)	

Nutrients per serving
Calories: 418
Protein: 4.2 g
Carbohydrate: 59.8 g
Fat: 19.2 g

- Preheat oven to 350°F (180°C).
- In a medium bowl, stir together eggs, corn syrup, sugar, melted butter and vanilla until well blended. Stir in pecans, cranberries and orange rind. Pour into pastry shell.
- Bake 50 to 55 minutes or until knife inserted halfway between center and edge comes out clean. (If edge of pie browns too quickly, protect with foil.)
- Cool on a wire rack. Serve with whipped cream, if desired.

1

For a decorative effect, place a doily on top of the cake.

2

Sprinkle with icing sugar.

3

Remove the doily carefully.

Best Chocolate Pound Cake

Makes 20 servings
Preparation: 12 minutes
Cooking: 55 minutes
Standing: 8 hours

2/3 cup	unsweetened cocoa	150 mL
2 3/4 cups	all-purpose flour	675 mL
1 tsp	baking powder	5 mL
1/2 tsp	salt	2 mL
1 cup	butter or margarine, softened	250 mL
1/2 cup	mayonnaise	125 mL
2 1/2 cups	sugar	625 mL
1 tsp	vanilla extract	5 mL
5	eggs	5
1 cup	milk	250 mL

- Preheat oven to 325°F (160°C).
- Grease and flour a 10-inch (25 cm) tube pan or Bundt pan, or two 9 x 5-inch (23 x 13 cm) loaf pans.
- In a small bowl, sift cocoa. Stir in flour, baking powder and salt. Set aside.
- In a large mixing bowl, beat butter and mayonnaise until smooth. Gradually beat in sugar; beat at high speed until light and fluffy, about 3 minutes. Blend in vanilla. Add eggs, one at a time, beating well after each addition. Stir in small quantities of flour mixture and milk alternately, beginning and ending with flour. Spread in prepared pan.
- Bake 55 to 65 minutes for loaf pans, or 75 to 85 minutes for tube or Bundt pan, or until wooden toothpick inserted in center comes out clean.
- Cool in pan on wire rack 10 minutes. Loosen cake from pan and remove. Cool completely. Wrap in foil and let stand at least overnight.

TIPS: For a decorative effect, place a doily on top of cake and sprinkle with icing sugar. Remove doily carefully.

Serve with homemade custard sauce (see page 170).

Nutrients per serving
Calories: 315
Protein: 4.4 g
Carbohydrate: 40.3 g
Fat: 16.0 g

Mandarin Orange Cheesecake

Makes 12 servings
Preparation: 10 minutes
Cooking: 50 minutes
Refrigeration: 4 hours

Crust

	cooking spray	
1 cup	graham cracker crumbs	250 mL
3 tbsp	sugar	45 mL
1/4 cup	melted butter or margarine	50 mL

Cake

2	8-oz (250 g) packages regular or light Cream cheese, softened	2
3/4 cup	sugar	175 mL
1/4 cup	cornstarch	50 mL
3	eggs	3
2 tsp	vanilla extract	10 mL
2	10-oz (284 mL) cans mandarin orange sections, divided	2
1/2 cup	mandarin syrup	125 mL
1 cup	liquid (mandarin syrup plus orange juice)	250 mL
1/4 cup	sugar	50 mL
4 tsp	cornstarch	20 mL

small grape clusters and mint leaves, for garnish (optional)

- Preheat oven to 325°F (160°C).

Crust

- Spray sides of an 8½-inch (21 cm) spring-form pan with cooking spray. In a bowl, combine graham cracker crumbs, sugar and melted butter or margarine. Press into pan. Refrigerate.

Cake

- In a blender or food processor, combine Cream cheese, sugar, cornstarch, eggs and vanilla.

- Drain 1 can of mandarin sections; add 1/2 cup (125 mL) syrup to Cream cheese mixture. Blend 1 minute or until smooth, scraping down sides once. Chop drained mandarin sections; stir into filling. Pour over crust.

- Bake 50 to 60 minutes or until set. Turn oven off, open door slightly and let cheesecake cool in the oven 1 hour. Remove to a wire rack and cool completely. Remove sides of pan.

- Drain remaining can of orange sections. Add enough orange juice to syrup to make 1 cup (250 mL) liquid. In a small saucepan, combine sugar, cornstarch, and syrup/juice mixture. Bring to a boil over medium heat, stirring constantly. Simmer 2 minutes.

- Spoon half of orange mixture over cake. Arrange orange sections on top and spoon remaining mixture over cake. Refrigerate at least 4 hours. Garnish with small grape clusters and mint leaves, if desired.

Nutrients per serving
Calories: 348
Protein: 5.7 g
Carbohydrate: 36.2 g
Fat: 20.9 g

Fruit Salad with Honey Lime Dressing

Try other fruits that are in season, topped with this tangy dressing.

Makes 6 servings
Preparation: 5 minutes
Cooking: 5 minutes

1	10-oz (284 mL) can mandarin orange sections, drained	1
2 cups	strawberries, halved	500 mL
2 cups	cubed melon (honeydew or cantaloup)	500 mL
2	medium bananas, sliced	2

Honey Lime Dressing

3	eggs, well beaten	3
1/2 cup	liquid honey	125 mL
1/4 cup	lime juice	50 mL
1 cup	sour cream	250 mL

- In a large bowl, combine mandarin oranges, strawberries, melon and bananas and toss well. Cover and chill.
- In a saucepan, combine eggs, honey and lime juice. Cook, stirring, over low heat until mixture comes to a boil and thickens. Cool. Fold in sour cream. Chill. Makes 2 cups (500 mL) dressing.
- Just before serving, pour dressing over fruit; toss until fruit is well coated.

TIP: To make dressing in the microwave, combine eggs, honey, and lime juice in a medium-size microwaveable bowl. Microwave at 'Medium-high' (70%) 5 to 6 minutes, until mixture just comes to a boil and thickens. Cool. Fold in sour cream.

Nutrients per serving
Calories: 277
Protein: 5.6 g
Carbohydrate: 49.6 g
Fat: 8.4 g

Individual Custards

Makes 4 servings
Preparation: 5 minutes
Cooking: 8 minutes

3	eggs	3
1½ cups	milk	375 mL
½ tsp	vanilla extract	2 mL
¼ cup	sugar	50 mL
	pinch salt (optional)	
	dash nutmeg	

- In a 4-cup (1 L) glass bowl, beat eggs, milk, vanilla, sugar and salt until sugar is dissolved.
- Pour into 4 6-oz (200 mL) glass custard cups. Sprinkle each with nutmeg.
- Microwave on 'Medium' (50%) 8 to 12 minutes, rotating the custard cups once or twice. Remove custards as they are done. Continue cooking remaining custards.
- Allow custards to cool completely or until set, then chill.

TIP: Delicate custards continue to cook with internal heat after microwaving. To test for doneness, shake each custard gently. The center should quiver like soft-set gelatin. A knife inserted between the center and edge will not come out clean when custard is done. Rely on standing time to set the custard. Remove custards as they are done. Test remaining ones frequently as they will cook faster with less food in the microwave.

Nutrients per serving
Calories: 151
Protein: 7.7 g
Carbohydrate: 17.5 g
Fat: 5.5 g

151

Meringue Trifle

A special trifle of crunchy meringue, bananas and rich chocolate in custard. This recipe looks long but the steps are simple—and well worth it!

Makes 8 servings
Preparation: 15 minutes
Baking time: 2 hours

Meringue

4	egg whites	4
	pinch cream of tartar	
1 cup	sugar	250 mL
1/2 tsp	vanilla extract	2 mL

Custard Sauce

1 cup	sugar	250 mL
1/4 cup	all-purpose flour	50 mL
	dash salt	
3 cups	milk	750 mL
4	egg yolks	4
2 tsp	vanilla extract	10 mL

Layers

3 tbsp	orange liqueur (optional)	45 mL
1 cup	whipped cream	250 mL
3	1-oz (28 g) squares semi-sweet chocolate	3
1 tbsp	butter	15 mL
3	large bananas	3

Nutrients per serving
Calories: 506
Protein: 8.2 g
Carbohydrate: 76.7 g
Fat: 20.3 g

- Preheat oven to 250°F (120°C).

Meringue

- In a bowl, beat egg whites with cream of tartar until soft peaks form. Gradually add sugar; continue beating until stiff, glossy peaks form. Beat in vanilla. Spoon mixture onto foil-lined baking sheet and spread evenly over pan. Bake 2 hours. Cool.

Custard Sauce

- In a saucepan, combine sugar, flour and salt. Add milk and egg yolks. Cook over medium-high heat, stirring constantly, until mixture comes to a boil and thickens. Remove from heat and add vanilla. Cool.

Assembling Layers

- Fold orange liqueur, if using, into whipped cream. Fold half of the whipped cream into the custard. In a small saucepan, melt chocolate and butter over low heat. Cut bananas into 1/2-inch (1 cm) slices.

- Spoon half of the custard into a 10-cup (2.5 L) serving bowl. Break meringue into pieces, about 1 to 2 inches (2.5 to 5 cm) in size. Spread half of the meringue pieces over custard and drizzle with one-third of the chocolate. Cover with half of the bananas. Repeat with layers of custard, meringue pieces, chocolate and bananas. Top with whipped cream and meringue crumbs, then remaining chocolate. Decorate with additional banana slices if desired. Refrigerate until ready to serve.

TIPS: Meringue may be prepared in advance and stored in an airtight container at room temperature or in the freezer.

Assemble the trifle no longer than 3 to 4 hours before serving, or meringue will become soft.

1

Spoon half of the custard into a serving bowl. Cover with half of the meringue pieces, a third of the chocolate and half of the bananas.

2

Repeat with layers of custard, meringue pieces, chocolate and bananas.

3

Top with whipped cream and meringue crumbs, then remaining chocolate.

153

Ambrosia Crepes

Makes 9 servings (2 crepes per serving)
Preparation: 15 minutes
Cooking: 20 minutes
Refrigeration: 1 hour

Crepes

3	eggs	3
1/2 tsp	salt	2 mL
1 cup	all-purpose flour	250 mL
11/2 cups	milk	375 mL
3 tbsp	melted butter, cooled	45 mL

Ambrosia Filling

1	19-oz (540 mL) can pineapple tidbits, well drained	1
2	10-oz (284 mL) cans mandarin orange segments, drained, or 11/2 cups (375 mL) halved orange segments	2
1/2 cup	sweetened flaked coconut	125 mL
3/4 cup	orange, lemon or vanilla flavored firm yogurt	175 mL
	fresh fruit and yogurt, for garnish	
	maple syrup (optional)	

Nutrients per serving
Calories: 226
Protein: 6.4 g
Carbohydrate: 33.1 g
Fat: 8.2 g

Crepes

- In a medium bowl, whisk together eggs and salt. Whisk in flour, milk and butter until smooth. Cover and refrigerate for at least 1 hour.

- Stir batter before using. Heat a 7- or 8-inch (17 or 20 cm) crepe pan or skillet until very hot. (It is ready when a few drops of water skitter across the pan and evaporate quickly.) Grease pan or skillet lightly with oil or shortening.

- Raise pan from heat with one hand and, with the other hand, pour about 3 tbsp (45 mL) batter into pan all at once. As you pour, tilt pan several times so that batter forms a thin film over bottom. Cook over medium heat until top is set, about 30 seconds. Loosen edges, turn over and cook a few seconds.

- Lift cooked crepe with spatula; place on wire rack to cool. Repeat procedure until all batter is used.

Filling

- In a bowl, combine all ingredients. Chill to blend flavors. Place about 1/4 cup (50 mL) filling on each crepe and fold as desired. Garnish with fresh fruit and yogurt. Drizzle with maple syrup, if desired.

TIP: Crepes can be made ahead of time and frozen. Stack cooled crepes with sheets of waxed paper between each. Place cooled crepe stack in freezer bag and freeze until needed.

1

Pour caramelized mixture into an 8-inch (20 cm) round baking dish, tilting pan to cover bottom.

2

Pour egg mixture into pan over caramel mixture.

3

Place in a pan of boiling water and bake until mixture is set.

Orange Crème Caramel

Makes 8 servings
Preparation: 15 minutes
Cooking: 50 minutes
Refrigeration: overnight

1 cup	sugar, divided	250 mL
1/4 cup	water	50 mL
5	eggs	5
2 1/2 cups	hot milk	625 mL
1 tbsp	grated orange rind	15 mL
1 tsp	vanilla extract	5 mL

- Preheat oven to 350°F (180°C).

- In a small heavy saucepan, combine half the sugar and the water. Cook over medium heat, stirring constantly, until sugar is dissolved. (Do not let mixture boil while stirring.)

- Increase heat to medium-high and boil, without stirring, until mixture caramelizes and is golden in color, 6 to 8 minutes. Pour immediately into an 8-inch (20 cm) round baking dish, tilting pan to cover bottom.

- In a bowl, whisk eggs with remaining sugar until blended. Stir in hot milk, orange rind and vanilla. Avoid overmixing. Pour into pan over caramel mixture.

- Place in a pan of boiling water and bake until mixture is set, 40 to 45 minutes.

- Remove from hot water. Cool on a rack. Cover with foil or plastic wrap and refrigerate overnight.

- To remove from mold, run a spatula carefully around custard. Invert a rimmed serving plate over custard and turn over. Serve in wedges.

TIPS: To eliminate air bubbles in the baked custard, let egg mixture rest 5 minutes before pouring over caramel.

This crème caramel can be prepared up to 2 days in advance. When cooled, cover tightly with plastic wrap or foil and keep refrigerated. Remove from mold up to 2 hours before serving and return to refrigerator.

Nutrients per serving
Calories: 183
Carbohydrate: 29.2 g
Protein: 6.4 g
Fat: 4.6 g

Apple Cheese Omelet

Makes 1 serving
Preparation: 10 minutes
Cooking: 10 minutes

1 tsp	butter	5 mL
1/2	apple, peeled, cored and thinly sliced	1/2
2 tsp	sugar, divided	10 mL
	cinnamon, to taste	
2	eggs	2
1 tsp	water	5 mL
2 tbsp	shredded Cheddar or Swiss cheese	30 mL
	cinnamon sugar or icing sugar (optional)	

Nutrients per serving
Calories: 307
Protein: 16.1 g
Carbohydrate: 19.1 g
Fat: 18.5 g

- In an 8-inch (20 cm) nonstick skillet with sloping sides, melt butter over medium heat. Add apple slices in one layer. Cook 2 minutes. Sprinkle with 1 tsp (5 mL) sugar and cinnamon, to taste. Cook until tender, 3 to 5 minutes longer.

- In a small bowl, combine eggs, 1 tsp (5 mL) sugar and water. Beat with a fork until eggs are just blended. Pour over apples in skillet.

- Stir with a spatula to allow egg mixture to cover bottom of pan. Use spatula to gently push cooked portions to the center, tilting skillet to allow uncooked egg to flow into empty spaces.

- When egg is almost set on surface, sprinkle cheese over half of omelet. Slip spatula under unfilled side, fold over filling and slide onto serving plate. Sprinkle with cinnamon or icing sugar, if desired, and serve immediately.

IT'S A PARTY!

Entertaining should be fun, eggciting and...easy! These festive recipes and decorations are sure to impress your guests.

Egg Tacos

Makes 4 servings
Preparation: 10 minutes
Cooking: 5 minutes

8	taco shells	8
8	eggs	8
1/2 cup	milk	125 mL
	salt and pepper, to taste	
2 cups	shredded lettuce	500 mL
2	tomatoes, diced	2
1 cup	shredded Monterey Jack or Cheddar cheese	250 mL
	salsa and sour cream (optional)	

- Heat taco shells as directed on package.

- In a bowl, beat together eggs, milk, salt and pepper.

- Heat a medium nonstick skillet over medium-high heat until hot enough to make a drop of water sizzle. Pour in egg mixture and immediately reduce heat to medium-low.

- As mixture begins to set, gently move spatula across bottom and sides of skillet to form large, soft curds. Cook until eggs are thickened but still moist, and no visible liquid remains, about 1 minute.

- Divide egg mixture among taco shells. Garnish as desired with lettuce, tomato, cheese, salsa and sour cream.

Nutrients per serving
Calories: 416
Protein: 23.1 g
Carbohydrate: 21.9 g
Fat: 26.0 g

Eggritos

Makes 3 servings
Preparation: 10 minutes
Cooking: 15 minutes

6	eggs	6
3/4 cup	corn kernels, frozen or canned	175 mL
1/4 cup	diced onion	50 mL
1/4 cup	diced green or red pepper	50 mL
1/4 cup	salsa	50 mL
1/4 tsp	dried basil	1 mL
1/4 tsp	oregano	1 mL
	salt and pepper, to taste	
1 tbsp	butter	15 mL
6	6-inch (15 cm) flour or whole wheat tortillas	6
6 tbsp	salsa	90 mL

Nutrients per serving
Calories: 440
Protein: 20.0 g
Carbohydrate: 49.0 g
Fat: 18.4 g

- In a medium bowl, lightly beat eggs. Add corn, onion, pepper, 1/4 cup (50 mL) salsa, basil, oregano, salt and pepper.

- In a 6-inch (15 cm) nonstick skillet melt 1/2 tsp (2 mL) butter over medium-high heat. Pour in 1/3 cup (75 mL) egg mixture. As eggs begin to set, lift edges to allow the uncooked egg to flow under.

- When omelet is set, slide onto a tortilla. Spread omelet with 1 tbsp (15 mL) salsa. Roll up.

- Repeat to make 5 more *eggritos*. Slice in half or into bite-size pieces. Serve hot or at room temperature.

TIP: For a lunch bag, cool *eggritos* completely. Cover separately in plastic wrap and refrigerate. To reheat, remove plastic wrap, roll one *eggrito* in paper napkin and reheat in microwave oven on 'High' (100%) 45 to 60 seconds.

Deviled Egg Dip

Makes 2 1/2 cups (625 mL)
Preparation: 5 minutes

1/2 cup	mayonnaise	125 mL
2 tbsp	lemon juice	30 mL
2 tsp	prepared mustard	10 mL
1/4 tsp	hot pepper sauce	1 mL
1/2 tsp	salt	2 mL
6	hard-cooked eggs, peeled	6
4 oz	whipped Cream cheese with onion	125 g
	parsley (optional)	

- Place mayonnaise, lemon juice, mustard, hot pepper sauce and salt in a blender container. Add one egg, cover and blend well. Continue adding eggs one at a time, blending after each addition, until mixture is smooth and light. Blend in whipped Cream cheese.

- Spoon dip into bowl; chill. Garnish with parsley, if desired, and serve with assorted crackers or raw vegetable sticks.

Nutrients per tablespoon
Calories: 42
Protein: 1.1 g
Carbohydrate: 0.5 g
Fat: 3.9 g

Pizza Omelet

Makes 4 servings
Preparation: 5 minutes
Cooking: 8 minutes

6	eggs	6
1/3 cup	water	75 mL
1/2 tsp	salt	2 mL
1/4 tsp	crushed oregano	1 mL
	pinch pepper	
1 tbsp	butter or margarine	15 mL
1/4 cup	pizza sauce	50 mL
1/2 cup	shredded Mozzarella cheese	125 mL
	sliced red pepper and olives (optional)	

- Preheat broiler.
- In a bowl, mix eggs, water, salt, oregano and pepper with a fork.
- In a 10-inch (25 cm) omelet pan or skillet with ovenproof handle, heat butter until pan is just hot enough to make a drop of water sizzle.

- Pour in egg mixture. Eggs should set at edges at once.
- With a spatula, carefully draw cooked portions at edges toward center so uncooked egg can flow under.
- Tilt skillet as necessary to hasten flow of uncooked egg.
- Slide pan back and forth rapidly over heat to keep mixture in motion and sliding freely.
- While top is still moist, spread with pizza sauce and sprinkle with cheese.
- Broil until cheese melts, if desired, or cover skillet and let stand until cheese is melted.
- With a spatula, slide pizza from pan onto serving plate. Garnish with sliced red pepper and olives, if desired. To serve, cut into wedges.

Nutrients per serving
Calories: 187
Protein: 12.6 g
Carbohydrate: 2.4 g
Fat: 13.9 g

*Egg*imals

Food Needed: Hard-cooked eggs (peeled), baby pickles, carrots, celery, cheese, cheese slices, cherry tomatoes, corn chips, cucumber, green onion, green pepper, lettuce, olives, etc.

Equipment Needed: Cutting board, knife and toothpicks.

*Egg*opotamus (Hippopotamus)

Use 2 hard-cooked eggs. Cut a large wedge out of one egg to form a mouth. Attach small pieces of celery to pieces of a toothpick and put in place as teeth. Make eyes from celery and cucumber slices; attach with toothpicks. Join head and body with a toothpick.

*Egg*alator (Alligator)

Use 2 hard-cooked eggs. Cut a zigzag pattern for teeth in first egg. Attach pieces of celery and green pepper for eyes. Make a slit in second egg and fill with a row of corn chips. Add pickles for feet and tail. Put head and body together with a toothpick.

P*egg*s (Pigs)

For feet, cut a large chunk of cheese into 4 small cubes. Set hard-cooked egg lengthwise on cubes of cheese. Cut out a round piece of cheese and use for a nose. Attach with a toothpick to the front of the pig (small end of egg). Use a small curly piece of green onion for a tail. Make eyes, ears and mouth out of cucumbers. Attach tail, eyes, ears and mouth with parts of a toothpick.

*Egg*apus (Octopus)

For the body, cut a thick slice from the small end of a hard-cooked egg. Cut 8 wiggly legs from a cheese slice. Arrange on a plate and set body on top. Make eyes from pieces of celery and pickle. Use a piece of pickle for a nose. Attach eyes and nose to head with part of a toothpick.

P*egg*uin (Penguin)

Cut a small slice off each end of a hard-cooked egg. Cut 2 thin slices from each side of a black olive for wings and 2 oval slices from another olive for feet. Attach wings to each side of egg, using small pieces of a toothpick. Arrange feet near body. Make eyes and nose from a cheese slice. Attach to black olive head with toothpicks. Set head on body and use toothpick to secure.

Sailboat Eggs

Kids will love these little "sailboats"! They make a great table decoration that can be eaten.

Makes 8 pieces
Preparation: 5 minutes

4	hard-cooked eggs, peeled	4
4	slices processed cheese	4
8	straight pretzels or toothpicks	8

- Slice eggs in half lengthwise. If necessary, trim a little egg white from the bottom of each egg half so that the sailboats are level.
- Slice cheese in half diagonally (to make two triangles).
- For each sailboat, use a pretzel and cheese triangle to make a mast and sail. Cheese may need to be trimmed.

TIP: Serve on a big platter with lettuce, raw vegetables and dip.

Nutrients per piece
Calories: 93
Protein: 6.3 g
Carbohydrate: 2.2 g
Fat: 6.4 g

Pineapple Dream Squares

Makes 16 squares
Preparation: 10 minutes
Cooking: 60 minutes

Base

	cooking spray	
1½ cups	all-purpose flour	375 mL
¼ cup	brown sugar, lightly packed	50 mL
½ cup	butter or margarine, softened	125 mL

Topping

3	eggs	3
1 cup	flaked coconut	250 mL
¾ cup	brown sugar, lightly packed	175 mL
¾ cup	corn syrup	175 mL
1	14-oz (398 mL) can crushed pineapple, well drained	1
2 tbsp	butter or margarine, melted	30 mL
1 tsp	vanilla extract	5 mL

Nutrients per serving
Calories: 273
Protein: 2.8 g
Carbohydrate: 41.0 g
Fat: 11.6 g

- Preheat oven to 350°F (180°C).

Base
- Spray a 9-inch (23 cm) square pan with cooking spray. In a medium bowl, combine flour and brown sugar. Cut in butter until mixture is crumbly. Press into pan.
- Bake until lightly browned, 12 to 15 minutes. Cool slightly.

Topping
- In a medium bowl, whisk eggs just until blended. Stir in remaining ingredients. Spread over base.

- Bake until topping is set but still soft in center, 40 to 45 minutes.
- Cool completely on a wire rack. Cut into squares. Keep refrigerated.

Variation: Melt 2 1-oz (28 g) squares semi-sweet chocolate and combine with 1 tsp (5 mL) vegetable oil. Drizzle over cooled squares. Let chocolate set before cutting.

Cranberry Layer Cake Chantilly

Makes 12 servings
Preparation: 30 minutes
Cooking: 35 minutes

Cake

6	eggs	6
1 tsp	vanilla extract	5 mL
1 cup	sugar	250 mL
1 cup	all-purpose flour	250 mL
1 tsp	baking powder	5 mL

Filling

1 cup	sugar	250 mL
1 tbsp	cornstarch	15 mL
1/3 cup	water	75 mL
3 cups	fresh or frozen cranberries, chopped	750 mL
2 cups	diced peeled apples	500 mL
1½ cups	whipping cream	375 mL
2 tbsp	sugar	30 mL

Nutrients per serving
Calories: 336
Protein: 4.9 g
Carbohydrate: 51.0 g
Fat: 13.1 g

- Preheat oven to 350°F (180°C).

Cake

- Grease two 9-inch (23 cm) round cake pans and line bottoms with waxed paper.
- Break eggs into a large bowl; place over hot tap water for 5 minutes. Add vanilla. With electric mixer, beat eggs and vanilla on high speed until foamy. Add sugar gradually and beat until eggs are very light, about 3 minutes.
- In another bowl, combine flour and baking powder; stir into egg mixture in three additions. Divide batter between pans.
- Bake 20 to 25 minutes, or until cake springs back when touched in center.
- Cool on cake racks 5 minutes. Turn out of pans, peel off paper and cool completely.

Filling

- In a medium saucepan, combine sugar and cornstarch. Stir in water, cranberries and apples. Bring to a boil over medium heat, stirring. Cook until apples are tender and mixture is thick, 3 to 4 minutes. Remove from heat and cool.

- Slice each cake in 2 to make a total of 4 layers. Place one layer on a serving plate; top with 1/2 cup (125 mL) filling. Repeat with 2 more layers, placing the last layer on top of cake crust-side up. Spread remaining filling on top.
- Whip cream with sugar. Frost sides of cake with cream, and pipe a border on top. Refrigerate until ready to serve.

TIP: Cake layers can be prepared up to 2 months in advance and kept frozen, or 2 days in advance and kept refrigerated. Prepare the cranberry-apple filling up to 2 days in advance and keep refrigerated. Fill and frost up to 4 hours before serving.

Festive Cherry Almond Cake

An absolutely wonderful cake, served with a custard sauce.

Makes 10 servings
Preparation: 15 minutes
Cooking: 1 hour, 20 minutes

1 cup	maraschino cherries, quartered	250 mL
2 cups	all-purpose flour	500 mL
2 tbsp	ground almonds	30 mL
2 tsp	baking powder	10 mL
1/2 tsp	salt	2 mL
3/4 cup	butter, softened	175 mL
1 tsp	almond extract	5 mL
3/4 cup	sugar	175 mL
4	eggs	4
1/3 cup	sour cream	75 mL

Custard Sauce

1 cup	milk	250 mL
1 cup	10% cream	250 mL
6	egg yolks	6
1/4 cup	sugar	50 mL
1/2 tsp	vanilla extract	2 mL

- Preheat oven to 325°F (160°C).

Cake

- Grease a deep 8-inch (20 cm) round cake pan. Line bottom with waxed paper and grease again.
- Pat maraschino cherries dry. In a bowl, combine flour, ground almonds, baking powder and salt. Add cherries and toss until pieces are well coated; reserve.
- In another bowl, beat butter, almond extract and sugar until light and fluffy. Add eggs one at a time, beating well after each addition.
- Stir in dry ingredients in three additions, alternately with sour cream. Spread into prepared pan.
- Bake 1 1/4 to 1 1/2 hours, or until toothpick inserted in center comes out clean. Cool 10 minutes. Turn cake out and cool completely.

Custard Sauce

- Heat milk and cream, without boiling. In a bowl, beat egg yolks with sugar; stir in hot milk and cream gradually. In a saucepan, cook over medium heat until thickened. Do not let mixture boil, and stir constantly. Remove from heat. Stir in vanilla. Serve cold.

- To serve, spoon custard sauce over each serving of cake.

Nutrients per serving
Calories: 339
Protein: 5.7 g
Carbohydrate: 39.8 g
Fat: 17.7 g

Easy Chocolate Pavlova

Makes 8 servings
Preparation: 30 minutes
Cooking: 1¼ hours + drying
Refrigeration: 3 hours

Meringues

4	egg whites	4
½ tsp	vanilla extract	2 mL
¼ tsp	cream of tartar	1 mL
	pinch salt	
1 cup	sugar	250 mL

Filling

2 tbsp	cornstarch	30 mL
½ cup	sugar	125 mL
1½ cups	milk	375 mL
2	1-oz (28 g) squares unsweetened chocolate, chopped	2
4	egg yolks	4
½ tsp	vanilla extract	2 mL
	fruit, for garnish	

Nutrients per serving
Calories: 274
Protein: 5.7 g
Carbohydrate: 50.1 g
Fat: 7.3 g

- Preheat oven to 250°F (120°C).

Meringues

- Line two baking sheets with foil. Trace 8 3½-inch (9 cm) circles on foil.
- Place egg whites in a bowl and place bowl in warm water for 3 minutes; remove. Add vanilla, cream of tartar, salt and ¼ cup (50 mL) sugar. Beat with electric mixer until soft peaks form. Gradually add remaining sugar, 2 tbsp (30 mL) at a time, beating until sugar is completely dissolved and meringue is very stiff.
- Spoon meringue into circles on foil; spread with a spoon, building a rim.
- Bake 75 minutes or until meringues are crisp but not browned, and can be removed from foil. Turn oven off and leave meringues in the oven, with the door closed, 4 hours or overnight.

Filling

- In a medium saucepan, combine cornstarch and sugar. Stir in milk and chocolate. Bring to a boil over medium heat, stirring constantly, and cook 30 seconds.
- Beat half of the mixture into the egg yolks. Pour yolk mixture into saucepan. Cook, stirring, over low heat 1 minute, without letting it boil. Stir in vanilla.
- Transfer mixture to a bowl. Place a sheet of plastic wrap directly over filling and refrigerate until cold.
- Spoon cold filling into meringue shells. Cover with aluminum foil. Refrigerate 3 to 24 hours. Garnish with fruit before serving.

TIP: Meringues can be made ahead and stored in an airtight container in a cool place for several days. Filling can be prepared a day ahead.

Orange Meringue Cookies

These feathery, light cookies will satisfy any sweet tooth, yet they contain no fat.

Makes 30 cookies
Preparation: 10 minutes
Baking: 2 hours + drying

3	egg whites	3
1/4 tsp	cream of tartar	1 mL
1/2 cup	sugar	125 mL
1 tbsp	grated orange rind	15 mL

- Preheat oven to 200°F (100°C).
- In a large bowl, beat egg whites until foamy; add cream of tartar and beat until soft peaks form. Continue beating and add sugar, one spoonful at a time. Beat until mixture forms stiff, glossy peaks. Fold in orange rind.
- Drop tablespoons of meringue mixture onto foil-lined baking sheets.
- Bake 2 hours. Meringues will still be moist.
- Turn oven off and let meringue cookies dry in oven overnight.

TIP: To make an elegant dessert, break a few cookies into chunks and combine with yogurt and fresh berries. Serve in sherbet glasses.

Variations: Substitute 1 tbsp (15 mL) cocoa for orange rind.

Nutrients per serving:
Calories: 15
Protein: 0.3 g
Carbohydrate: 3.4 g
Fat: 0 g

Holiday Eggnog

Makes 16 servings
Preparation: 5 minutes
Cooking: 25 minutes
Refrigeration: 3 hours

6	eggs	6
1/2 cup	sugar	125 mL
4 cups	milk	1 L
2 tsp	vanilla extract	10 mL
1/2 cup	brandy (optional)	125 mL
2 cups	whipping cream	500 mL
	ground nutmeg	

- In a large heavy saucepan, beat eggs and sugar until well blended. Gradually stir in milk. Cook over medium-low heat, stirring constantly, until mixture is thick enough to coat a spoon, about 25 minutes.

- Pour custard into a large bowl. Stir in vanilla and brandy, if using. Chill bowl in ice water for a few minutes, stirring occasionally. Cover and refrigerate at least 3 hours or overnight.

- To serve, beat whipping cream until soft peaks form. Gently fold whipped cream into custard. Sprinkle lightly with nutmeg. Keep eggnog refrigerated or place bowl on a bed of ice. Use within 2 hours.

Nutrients per serving
Calories: 182
Protein: 5.0 g
Carbohydrate: 10.4 g
Fat: 13.5 g

Egg Blow Out

Once you have emptied eggshells, you can decorate them in many different ways!

- To empty an eggshell, begin by washing and drying the egg.

- Pierce both ends with a large needle. Slightly enlarge the hole at the small end of the egg. Push the needle well into the egg in order to break the yolk.

- Hold the egg over a bowl with the small end down. Blow into the hole at the opposite end until the white and yolk are removed.

- Rinse the shell with cold water and allow to dry completely. (Use the raw egg for an omelet, a quiche or scrambled eggs.)

Coloring Eggs

Food coloring, natural dyes, commercial egg dyes and water-based felt pens can all be used for coloring eggs.

TIPS: Tongs are a handy tool to use for dipping raw or hard-cooked eggs in water.

An easy way to color a blown egg is to thread a length of thin wire through the holes in each end of the eggshell. Bend the wire at one end so the egg won't slip off. This is a handy tool for dipping the egg in the dye and hanging it to dry. A cake rack is also useful for drying eggs.

Food Coloring Technique

1

Mix 3/4 cup (175 mL) water and 1 tsp (5 mL) vinegar with 1/4 tsp (1 mL) food coloring. For brighter color, add more food coloring.

2

Completely submerge the eggs until they are tinted the desired color, from 2 to 5 minutes.

3

Remove eggs from the dye and allow to dry before adding another color or continuing to decorate.

Egg Animals

Various animals can be made by using odds and ends found around the house, once you empty eggshells according to the instructions on page 176. Here are some ideas:

Owl: Color eggshell brown with dye or felt pen. Glue on a beak made of construction paper. Use two small stones for feet. Draw eyes with felt pen.

Bird: Dye eggshell blue. Glue on a beak made of construction paper, and wings and a tail made of tissue paper. Draw eyes with a felt pen.

Mouse: Glue large pink ovals of construction paper on eggshell for ears. Add a pipe cleaner tail; draw whiskers and eyes with a felt pen.

Pig: Dye eggshell pink. Glue on miniature marshmallows for 4 legs and a snout. Make a curly tail from a pipe cleaner. Draw eyes with a felt pen.

Fish: Dye eggshell green, or color it green with paint or a felt pen. Draw scales with a felt pen. Cut eyes, tail and fins from construction paper and glue on.

Play Dough Characters

Empty eggshells according to the instructions on page 176.

To prepare the play dough

Combine 1 cup (250 mL) table salt with 2 cups (500 mL) all-purpose flour. Stir in 1 cup (250 mL) cold water. With your hands, press dough into a smooth ball. Do not tint dough at this point.

To make the characters

Form the play dough into the shapes you want for the characters you are going to make. (See below for the shapes you will need to make the rabbits on this page.) Place the shapes in position on empty eggshells on an ungreased baking sheet, without using glue. Bake in a 275°F (140°C) oven for 2 hours. Let characters cool completely. Paint with acrylic paint. Let dry completely.

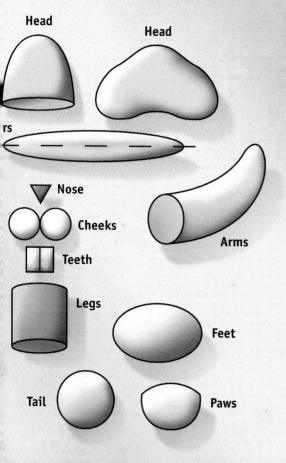

Head

Head

rs

Nose

Cheeks

Teeth

Arms

Legs

Feet

Tail

Paws

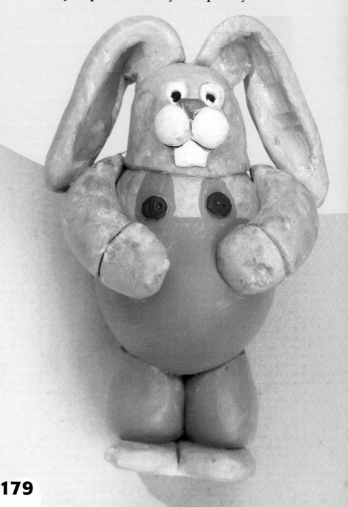

179

Christmas Tree Egg Ornaments

Empty the eggshells according to the instructions on page 176.

Reinforce the empty shells with two or three coats of flat white paint. Allow to dry before decorating.

Use your imagination to decorate these ornaments! You can color them using felt pens, latex or acrylic paint, or even spray paint. You can glue festive ribbons onto the eggs or write seasonal greetings on them.

The kids can draw a scene from their favorite Christmas story on their ornaments. Or you can have them write or draw their Christmas wish list on egg ornaments.

Why not make egg ornaments for everyone in the family? Write each family member's name on an egg using glitter or metallic markers.

To hang your ornaments on the Christmas tree, see instructions on page 185.

Santa Egg

Use a marker to draw Santa's eyes, nose and mouth. Glue on absorbent cotton for the beard and hair. Top the egg with a cone hat made of stiff red paper, with a tiny cotton ball on the end.

181

Egg & Noodle Fun

Empty the eggshells according to the instructions on page 176.

Using acrylic paint, cover the eggs with a uniform or patterned layer of color and allow to dry.

To make a design, use regular woodworking glue to paste a small amount of pasta, rice or beans on the eggs in the shape of a butterfly, star or flower. Allow to dry 30 minutes before painting the design.

Eggshell Mosaic

Recycle broken eggshells to create pretty mosaics.

- Rinse eggshells and break into tiny pieces.

- Prepare a variety of dye colors in plastic containers by adding a few drops of food coloring to a small amount of hot water. A drop of vinegar added to the water will help to set the color.

- To dye eggshells, simply immerse them in the water. Leaving the shells in the dye for varying lengths of time will create different shades of color to work with.

- Remove shells from dyes and spread them out on paper towels to dry. When shells are dry, gather the different colors in separate containers.

- The shell pieces should be arranged in the basic mosaic design before beginning to glue. When satisfied with your design, glue shell pieces into place with white glue. If desired, use a clear spray lacquer to coat the entire mosaic.

183

Gift Eggs

Empty eggshells according to the instructions on page 176.

Using clear acrylic glue, cover eggshells with small pieces of wrapping paper. Add a pretty bow.

Use leftover Christmas wrapping paper and ribbons to make pretty Christmas gift eggs. You can gather several of them together in a bowl to create a centerpiece for Christmas dinner.

These gift eggs could make an unusual addition to an egg collector's collection!

Hanging Eggs

Empty eggshells according to the instructions on page 176.

Cut a narrow ribbon or silk cord into 12-inch (30 cm) lengths. Fold in half and tie ends in a pretty bow or in a knot. Use a piece of floral wire or an embroidery hook to pull the folded end through the egg so that the bottom of the egg is resting on the bow. Hang eggs.

Another way to hang your eggs is to make a knot at the end of the ribbon. Thread the ribbon through the egg using a large needle. The egg will rest on the knot. Hang the egg and tie the ribbon to secure it.

To preserve your decorated eggs, apply a clear acrylic fixative, spray varnish or nail polish. For iridescent eggs, choose a pearlescent finish.

Egg Candles

These original candles will add ambiance to your dinner parties. Why not make one for each of your guests?

- Break and empty eggshells. Wash and dry shells, and color with acrylic craft paint, felt pens or dye. Decorate as desired.

- Spoon wax crystals into eggshells and position a wax-coated candlewick in the center of each egg. Wax crystals will melt after candles are lit and begin to burn.

- Prop candles up with sand, small decorative rocks or egg cups.

- Never leave lit candles unattended.

Egg Flower Vases

These tiny flower vases make a perfect table decoration for a springtime brunch.

- Carefully break the top third off the eggs; empty the eggs and wash and dry the shells. Dye, paint or decorate the eggs as desired.
- Prop the shells up with sand, modeling clay or suitably sized candle-holders.
- Fill the egg vases with water and place small flowers inside. In the spring you can use lily of the valley, bluebells and violets.

189

Index